W9-ARL-771

FIRE!

FIRE!

a play by

JOHN ROC

ATHENEUM New York

1969

CAUTION: *Professionals and amateurs are hereby warned that* FIRE!, *being fully protected under the copyright laws of the United States of America, the British Empire, including the Dominion of Canada, and all other countries of the Copyright Union, is subject to a royalty. All rights, including professional, amateur, motion pictures, recitation, public reading, radio and television broadcasting and the rights of translation in foreign languages are strictly reserved. Amateurs may give stage production of this play upon payment of royalty of Fifty Dollars for the first performance and Twenty-Five Dollars for each additional performance one week before the play is to be given to Samuel French, Inc., at 25 West 45th St., New York, N. Y. 10036, or 7623 Sunset Blvd., Hollywood, Calif., or if in Canada to Samuel French (Canada) Ltd., at 27 Grenville St., Toronto, Ont. All other rights apply to Henderson/Scott, Ltd., 850 Seventh Ave., New York, N. Y. 10019.*

Copyright © 1969 by John Roc
All rights reserved
Library of Congress catalog card number 69–15511
Published simultaneously in Canada by McClelland and Stewart Ltd.
Manufactured in the United States of America by H. Wolff, New York
Designed by Kathleen Carey
First Edition

TO

KATHERINE AND RICHARD

WHO FED ME

IN A MULTITUDE OF WAYS

FIRE! was first presented at the Brandeis University Theatre, Waltham, Massachusetts, May 1, 1968, with the following cast:

LORNA	*Robyn Lee Goodman*
JASON	*Peter MacLean*
RONALD	*Roy K. Stevens*
STANLEY	*Matt Conley*
WALTER	*Mervyn Williams*
DELIA	*Janet Ross*
SARAH	*Vanya Franck*
MARCO	*David Howard*

Direction by Charles Werner Moore
Setting and Lighting by Christopher Idoine
Costumes by Barbara Cox

FIRE! was subsequently presented by David Black, in association with Jonathon Burrows, at the Longacre Theatre, New York City, on January 28, 1969, with the following cast:

LORNA	*Carolyn Coates*
JASON	*Peter MacLean*
RONALD	*Roy K. Stevens*
STANLEY	*Louis Edmonds*
WALTER	*John Wardwell*
DELIA	*Jennifer Darling*
SARAH	*Audra Lindley*
MARCO	*Rene Auberjonois*

Direction by Charles Werner Moore
Setting and Lighting by Howard Bay
Costumes by Lewis Brown

FIRE!

ACT ONE

*Before the curtain rises, the sound of Bach, on a harp-
sichord. The curtain rises in darkness. Bach changes
to electronic music which, in turn, becomes the lilting
melody of a sweet soprano voice singing la-las, half lul-
laby, half threnody. Then, softly, the whispering of a
man and woman and their low laughter, as if after love-
making. The lullaby-lamentation again, then:*

Out of the darkness, LORNA *appears. She is in her mid-
thirties, ugly and beautiful. She wears the detritus of
splendor—velvet, satin, cloth of gold, in rags; a broken
coronet, bejeweled with glass and rhinestones; brilliant
colors, gone to shame. She's in a terror as she comes
down to speak directly to the audience.*

LORNA

You! You didn't give me half a chance, did you? I ran
as fast as I could—but I didn't have a chance! You know
as well as I do that I need a long head start, or he'll catch
me!—a *long* head start! Why, if I leave anything behind
me—the faintest trail—he's there! He can catch me by
the echo of my voice! (*With intensity*) No, it's not true
that I *want* him to catch me—it's not true! I run as fast

as I ever can! And if that's *too* fast it doesn't mean *I'm* trying to catch up with *him!* Round and round and round! You tell me—I don't know—you tell me *what's the proper pace?!*

(*Silence. As if already sensing his presence, she goes still. A thin sound of music. Silence again. Then, in the dark, barely discernible,* JASON's *face. He is handsome, driven, worn. There is the suggestion of a uniform about his clothes. His hungers are deep.*)

JASON

Take a breath. Don't run any more. I won't hurt you.

LORNA

Please. Go away.

JASON

Why do you think I'll hurt you?

LORNA *(Wryly)*

You don't suppose I'd stop to *think* why you'd hurt me?

JASON

It's worth a thought. Have I *ever* hurt you?

LORNA

I've never been dead either.

JASON *(With a smile)*

How long can *that* stay true?

4

LORNA

Jason, go away.

JASON

I'm the only one who's ever made love to you by day-light. Did that hurt you?

LORNA

Go away.

JASON

The world is round. What difference does it make who catches whom?

LORNA

I just said that to them—you're an eavesdropper. Round and round, I said.

JASON

And if it's flat, you'll run right off the edge. I need you, Lorna. It'll be morning soon. I'll need you badly, when the others come.

LORNA

I won't be there.

JASON

Yes you will. (*He strikes a match in the darkness.*) What's the name of this?

LORNA

I won't be there!

5

JASON

The name, that's all—the name!

LORNA

It's a match.

JASON

Come on. Play fair.

LORNA

A light!

JASON

Damn you, Lorna, is it always two forward and three
back?! If it's only a light, it's nothing! What can it
illuminate?—a tiny pocket in the dark?—who cares?
There's still the outer black. Horrors, furies, succubi! A
light?—what good?—brighten the corner where you
are? . . . No . . . Demons. (*He blows out the match.*)
Please—we try again. (*He lights another match.*) What's
this?

LORNA

It's a . . . light.
   (*Slowly, he starts toward her with the lighted
   match.*)
No—please don't!—it's fire!
                    (*He stops.*)

JASON

Again.

6

LORNA

Fire.

JASON (*Gently*)

It's morning now. The others are arriving.

LORNA

You haven't caught me, Jason.

JASON

You've caught *me*, Lorna. Come.
> (*The lights come up to reveal the full stage.*
> RONALD *enters. He is in his late teens with the*
> *studied innocence of an eight-year-old. He car-*
> *ries a pouch at his side. It is filled with a num-*
> *ber of hand toys—little tools, finger puppets,*
> *puzzles. From time to time, he totally absents*
> *himself and plays with them. Right now, he*
> *holds a lead which trails, dogless, behind him.*)

RONALD

Am I late?

JASON

No, Ronald. You're early.

RONALD

If I go out and come in again, will I be on time?

JASON

You're on time now, Ronald.

7

RONALD

If I go out and come in again, will I be early or late?

JASON

You'll be later, but not late.

RONALD *(Shrewdly)*

If I come *much* later, I won't be later any more, I'll be late.

JASON

Yes, Ronald.

RONALD

I'm certainly glad we straightened *that* out—I thought we never would. May I bring my dog to the meeting?

JASON

You haven't any dog, Ronald.

RONALD

May I bring the dog I haven't got?

JASON

It's a difficult question. I'll think about it.

RONALD

He's housebroken and well trained. He's better trained than many of the people who'll be here. May I bring my little dog?

8

JASON

Yes, Ronald.

RONALD (*Shrewd again*)

You're really quite corrupt, aren't you? If you think you'll get my vote by letting me bring the dog I haven't got, you're mightily mistaken.

JASON (*With a smile*)

Am I?

RONALD

Mightily! (*To* LORNA) How much do you like me?—how much?

LORNA

In round numbers?

RONALD

Enough to hold my head?

LORNA

I think enough for that.

JASON

Hands off!

RONALD (*To* JASON)

You hold it then.
> (STANLEY *enters. He wears brilliant clothes and a leather belt as wide as a cummerbund, vividly painted. He is effete.*)

STANLEY

Are we holding his head again?

RONALD

Not you, Stanley.

STANLEY

You don't know what you're missing. I'm good at it.
I've held a lot of heads in my day, one way or another.
Why, last night alone, I went into the city—and held
a lot of heads! A lovely night last night! I did all the
things one does in town! I peeked through a dozen key-
holes. I found a cockroach and ate it. I urinated on a cat.

LORNA

The evening was routine. Which city did the sweet lad
say?

STANLEY

Is this unsavory tart going to be uppity with me today?

LORNA

Uppity, downity, he went to townity.

STANLEY

Vomity.

RONALD

Want to pat my puppy, Stanley?

STANLEY

Certainly—stand up.
    (WALTER *enters. He is in his late fifties. He is*

dressed in black except for the following: His collar is white, stiff and easily detached so that, at will, it can be turned into a clerical one. When he does this, he quickly discards his flowered tie which snaps off easily. He wears one emerald green shoe. And he carries a huge disreputable suitcase with a multitude of labels on it. WALTER *is now in a flurry of busy-ness and consequentiality.*)

WALTER

I hope I'm not late. I missed the express this morning and I never take the local—I'd rather walk. I did walk. Ninety-three miles from dawn to breakfast. Damn foreign timetables—can't make them out! And the natives don't speak a word of their own language—so where are we? Is this going to be another one of those inconclusive meetings?

JASON

Depends on you, Walter.

WALTER

Why me? I'm willing—as usual and as always—to accept any conclusion unanimously arrived at.

STANLEY

That's as good as a belch in the wind.

WALTER

I didn't make up that rule about unanimity. (*Pointing to* JASON) He did.

JASON

Did I really?

WALTER

Yes, you did! "Everybody" you said. "Let's have everybody!"

LORNA (*Quietly*)

No. What he said was: "I *want* everybody!"

JASON (*With a smile*)

Did I say that?

> (DELIA *enters. She is nubile and craving. She wears enough clothes to bedeck three women, each piece chosen with zealous attention to bizarre detail. One orange-colored stocking; the other fuchsia—a mask at the end of a stick—shoes, unmatched, that glitter and gleam—fingernails in ten different colors. And hardly any of her person exposed—just an oval of face.*)

DELIA

I hope you all deserve to look at me!

JASON

Come in, Delia.

DELIA

I hope I'm not wasted on this crowd. Hours! I've spent hours in front of that mirror making myself irresistible. "But will they notice?" I said to myself, "Will they appreciate? The jewel on a shoe, the cut of a bodice, the color of a fingernail. Will they look? And if they look—have they the eyes to see?"

STANLEY

Aren't they wearing skirts longer this year?

DELIA

They're wearing tongues shorter. Stick yours out—I'll hem it for you! Don't I look ravishing?

LORNA

Go on, pussy—parade! Preen and parade.

DELIA

Not one of you—not a single one of you is dressed for the occasion. And one of you's in rags! (*She of course means* LORNA.)

LORNA (*Quietly*)

Get off my train.

DELIA (*Also quiet*)

Dressed in rags. Remainders. Remnants and residues. Candle ends and coffee grounds!

LORNA

Get off my train.

DELIA

In *rags!*

LORNA (*Very quietly*)

I am wearing a white satin dress. With a train . . .
diaphanous . . . in gold. Eyelet embroidery—done by
a thousand bleeding-fingered nuns. Flowers, these . . .
daisies, marigolds, bleeding hearts . . . And all my
jewels are red. . . . Garnets, rubies, bloodstones shot
with red. I am elegant. I am wearing a bloody, bleeding
dress! (*Then, with quietest warning*) Get off my train!

STANLEY

You'd better get off her train, puss.

DELIA (*Unnerved*)

No! She's not wearing that kind of dress—and there's
no train to it! And if there is, I'm across the room from
her and I'm not standing on it! And if I am, I'll be
damned if I move!

RONALD (*Not unkindly*)

I think you'll have to, Delia.

DELIA

No.

STANLEY

Get off the damn train!

DELIA

No!

WALTER

Delia, be reasonable. If you're on the wrong train, you

14

have to get off. If you're on a train without a ticket, you have to get off. If there isn't any train, you have to walk! One way or another—when you're where you shouldn't be, you have to go somewhere else! *You have to get off!*

DELIA (*In distress*)
No, no, no—you're all on her side—you're always on her side—and it gets warmer and warmer in here—I have to take some clothes off—(*Which she starts to do*) —and I will not get off her train—no!

JASON (*Quietly*)
You'll have to move, Delia.

DELIA
Jason, please!

JASON
Move, Delia. Get off!
(*A still instant.* DELIA *lifts her foot slowly— high—a movement that gets her off the train. The room goes merry.*)

EVERYBODY
You did that very nicely! . . . Brava, Delia, brava! . . . Congratulations. I want to congratulate both of you!

WALTER
Good—that's very good. Compromises—making peace —I'm glad to see that. Give a little, take a little. Get the other fellow's point of view!—meet him half way!

15

STANLEY

From which end of him do you suppose those sounds emanate?

WALTER

Look here, you! If you were all as adaptable as I am, we wouldn't be in this fix! Give a little, take a little! I believe in that! Wear two hats—your own and the other fellow's. Why, I even wear two collars! My own —and His! (*He turns his collar around so that it becomes the collar of a minister.*)

STANLEY (*To* DELIA)

Would you lend me your lipstick?

DELIA

Why?

STANLEY

I want to mark his collar "Front" and "Back."

LORNA

So God will know whether he's coming or going.

RONALD

When people say they don't know whether they're coming or going—which way do they want to go?

WALTER (*Irritably, to* RONALD)

They can't go anywhere, if they don't know where they've been or where they're bound!

16

RONALD (*Innocently*)
Are they bound?

LORNA
Not tightly.

STANLEY
Loosely.

LORNA
Slipknots.

STANLEY
They can get out easily.

RONALD
Out of where?

WALTER (*His irritation growing*)
Out of wherever they are!

RONALD
Into what?

DELIA
Into something cool and comfortable. (*And she starts to get out of another article of clothing.*) Oh, I'm stuck! Someone help me! I'm stuck!

STANLEY (*Bitchily*)
Nobody help her—let her rip her way out!

DELIA

Help me—somebody help me!

STANLEY

What, darling?—don't know your own geography? This peninsula here—it's your head. This is your arm, dear. It's supposed to go through that sleeve. (*Not helping her*) No, not that, darling—that's a leg.

DELIA

Help—help me!

STANLEY

And that's a buttock—you have two of them. I'd say that two is one too many. Wrong way, darling—cul de sac!—dead end!

DELIA

Help!—help! No—don't!—don't!

WALTER

He's tying her sleeves together!

DELIA

Stop him!

JASON   (*Moving in*)

Out of the way, Stanley.

STANLEY

Spoilsport.

18

(JASON *helps her to get untangled.*)

DELIA (*Starting for* STANLEY)
You bastard!

JASON
Enough!

STANLEY
No—let her come. Come on, duck!

JASON
Stop it—both of you! (*A moment.*) We'll have no more of that. Are we all here? Who's missing?

LORNA
Marco.

JASON
I thought you'd notice that.

WALTER
And Sarah. Sarah's missing.
(SARAH *enters. She is a middle-aged mother.*)

SARAH
Sarah's here.

WALTER
And looking well! Look how well she looks!

SARAH
Don't drivel, Walter.

19

WALTER

It is not drivel! I have the bright romantic eye! I see the beauty of women!

SARAH

I said don't drivel, wipe your chin! I'm padded to look older and more ample than I am. I'm wadded round my waist, three inches thick—and if you think these mammaries are mine, you're misinformed. I'm dressed in motherhood. It's an indignity. Where do I sit?

JASON

Right there, Sarah.

SARAH

What will I be required to do?

JASON

Just vote when the time comes.

SARAH

As a mother, will I be required to deliver a child? In public?

JASON

Uh . . . I don't think so, Sarah.

SARAH

That's a blessing. It's a bother giving birth to human beings—their skulls are too big. A man does no better with a big head than a bird does with a little one.

20

WALTER (*With a wink of approval*)
Next time, Sarah, you go ahead and have a nightingale.

STANLEY
A vulture, more likely.
(*There is a bristle in the atmosphere.* JASON
steps forward.)

JASON
It's getting late. We must begin.

LORNA
Without Marco?

JASON
You want him?—fetch him!

STANLEY
No—don't! (*To* JASON) You don't stand a chance if
Marco comes. Get started.

JASON
Unanimity.

STANLEY
What chance for unanimity if Marco's here?!

JASON
No choice or chance—we don't have either. We have
to wait.
(MARCO *appears. He is about* JASON'S *age, but*

21

*his strengths are harder to define. He is more
mercurial.*)
Not long. Come in, Marco.
(*In silence,* MARCO *moves into their midst. He
stands between* JASON *and* LORNA.)

DELIA (*Dithering*)
Marco! Marco, come sit by me, Marco!

RONALD
No—by me! I've saved a place for you!

LORNA (*Quietly*)
We thought you weren't coming.

MARCO
Not coming? I wouldn't miss the world for this meeting.

WALTER (*Cheerily*)
He means "the meeting for the world." (*To* MARCO—
with amiable helpfulness) That's the common expression, Marco. "I wouldn't miss the such-and-such for the
world." Whatever the such-and-such may be, "the
world" comes last! I think that's what you meant.

LORNA
I think he said what he meant.

MARCO (*Wryly, to* LORNA)
You're very kind. (*To* JASON) Shall we get on with it?

22

STANLEY

He enters last and wants to be the first to start.

JASON

That's leadership.

STANLEY

It's gall. (*To* MARCO) Did you know it's gall?

SARAH

He knows. Marco knows who he is.

JASON (*With a smile to* MARCO)

Do you, Marco?

MARCO (*Also smiling*)

I'm not sure. But if you lined us all up, I think I could pick myself out. A meeting, did you say?

JASON

Yes. We start. I've not been ready to state the question until today. I've hinted at it, nights. I've taken you aside —each one. And thought—each time—"This one—I've got this one!" This one, that one—him—her! But then— every dawn—each one of you went scurrying back into the darkness. Well, now it's daylight. (*With controlled excitement*) And I've got one of you.

MARCO

Which one? (*He looks from one to another in the room.*)

23

WALTER

Don't look at me. I didn't vote his way.

MARCO

Which one, Jason?

JASON

Not yet. I want this done quite properly. Nobody will say: "He caught me unaware." The question first.

MARCO

The question, then?

JASON

. . . Fire.

MARCO

It's not a question, it's an expletive.

RONALD (*With quiet alarm*)

What does it mean?

DELIA

Will there be pain in it?

WALTER

Point of protocol! It really should go into committee first, I think.

RONALD

May I go home?

24

JASON (*Gently*)

Certainly, Ronald. Go on.

(*They all tensely watch* RONALD *as he picks up his toys. He drops one, picks it up, drops another. At last, just as he has himself assembled and at the door, he stops. He cannot leave. He turns.*)

RONALD

Fire, did you say?

JASON (*Not unkindly*)

Yes, Ronald.

(RONALD *looks from one to another in the room. At last he stops at* WALTER.)

RONALD

Tell me.

WALTER (*Apprehensively*)

Tell you what?

RONALD (*Pleading*)

Tell me anything. I'll be grateful for anything.

WALTER

Go away.

RONALD

No—please.

WALTER (*Frightened*)

Fire's not anything—it's nothing at all!

STANLEY

Well, it's not here, certainly—and it's not hell and it's not heaven.

JASON (*Quietly*)

It could be.

WALTER

Could be what?

JASON

Prometheus.

RONALD

Is that heaven?

STANLEY

The devil it is!

WALTER (*Excited*)

That's it!—the devil it *is!* Fire is the devil! Look into the flame and you look into the eye of the devil! The expression is hellfire and *damnation*, not hellfire and *salvation!* Not on your life! *But!*—(*To* JASON)—did you say Prometheus? *Well!*—on the other hand—!

MARCO

Did you say you have an ally, Jason?—who? Which one?

26

JASON

You wouldn't care to guess?

MARCO

Is it a game, then? Like words?

JASON

A game like words—exactly! Care to start?

MARCO

Ibid.

JASON

That *is* a word! Caught you, right off! You can't avoid
a meaning, can you, boy?

MARCO

Start over! Sooka!

JASON

Mooka.

MARCO

Bellamirado.

JASON

Modelladoro.

MARCO

Stibe.

27

JASON

Libe.

MARCO

Noldin.

JASON

Arrapundra.

MARCO

Corralora.

JASON

Flibbo!

MARCO

Simulacrum!

JASON (*Catching him*)
Ha! Simulacrum!—that's a word!

MARCO

No!

JASON

A real word, yes!

MARCO

Not real!—only by resemblance!

JASON

The very meaning of the word: resemblance!

28

MARCO

Unreal—an image!

JASON

The very word, the word!

MARCO

I thought you said the word was fire!

JASON

Yes, I did!

MARCO

Ally! Which one is your ally?

JASON

Which do you think?

MARCO

Who?

JASON

You!

MARCO

I'm not your ally, Jason! Who is?

JASON

I didn't say!

MARCO

Fire's what you said, my friend! Fizgig and girandole—
suttee and Vulcan!

WALTER

Hosannah!

JASON

Burning Sabbath!

MARCO

Who's your ally!?

JASON

Bellamirado!

MARCO (*Turning quickly on* LORNA)
Is it you?

LORNA

No!

MARCO

What did he do for you last night? Was there a wind?

LORNA

He kissed me! He burned me with a match—no wind!

MARCO

Oh, I believe that!

30

LORNA

I'm not his ally!

MARCO

Who then? (*Whirling to the rest of the room*) Who's the convert?

STANLEY (*Quietly*)

I am. . . .

(*The room goes still.*)

MARCO (*An instant. He laughs.*)

Well, that's a relief! (*To* JASON) This the convert you're crowing about? Convert? Pervert!

STANLEY

Mind your tongue, Marco!

MARCO

You're for burning, are you?

STANLEY

Yes!

MARCO

What'd he give you to vote that way? What'd he promise? Let you pull the feathers out of a crippled bird?

STANLEY

Stop that!

31

MARCO

A lady's bandage?

STANLEY

You're disgusting!—stop it!

MARCO

Let you suck his soiled handkerchief?

STANLEY

Stop that!—stop! (*He rushes down to the audience.*)
Stop him! Don't let him talk like that! You let him use
those words and what's there left for *me* to say!? You've
left me little enough to protect myself with! A dash of
vitriol in the face!—a cloud of scurf in the eyes!—that's
all the weaponry I've got! And if you take them from
me and give them to every upright Dick and Harry—
why, I'm exposed and helpless! Now, give me muck to
throw! Guano!—give me guano! (*He turns back and
faces* MARCO *with strength. He says quietly*) You are
pus. You are pus and putrefaction.

MARCO

Say more.

STANLEY

Turds and jakes.

MARCO

Are you really his ally?

32

STANLEY

Excreta magna—cloaca maxima!

MARCO

Fire, Stanley?—do you mean it?—do you really?

STANLEY

Let me be!

MARCO

Answer me! Come out from out that hill of ordure!—
answer me!

MARCO (*As Stanley turns away*)

Look at me! Fire, did you say? You're too wet to burn!

STANLEY (*Hectic, in flight*)

Tinder! I'm dry as tinder!

MARCO

Wet, I say! With tears! Your bib was sopping wet last
night!

STANLEY

Me?—not me! I haven't cried in generations!

MARCO

Oh, let me tell you—all of you—he cried, he did! He
cried like a baby for every bygone pacifier! A pillow or
a prayerbook, a dirty old doll or a sugar tit! "Oh God,"
he cried, "oh mother!"

STANLEY

No—I did not!—no!

MARCO

(*Continuing through* STANLEY's *interruption*)
Oh father, oh friend!

STANLEY

Liar!—he's a liar!

MARCO

Too wet!—your desperation isn't dry enough!

STANLEY

Liar—liar!

MARCO

You'll never burn!

STANLEY

Stop it—let me be! (*He talks to the audience again.*) It's
not fair!—not fair to catch me behind my old perversions! I've run way past them! Why turn me back? I
don't *care* if that's what perversion is!—turn me some
way I haven't turned before! Is it always back? The rod,
the rope?—the billy and the knout, the crucifixion and
the corpse? The corpse should be the last!—why isn't
it?—when is resurrection time in the city morgue? Oh,
who's abusing me?—the man outside?—the man inside
my skin? Oh yes! In the end, it's as the old horny-handed
queen said: The master of us all is masturbation! So,
always—ever and always—the turn is back on me! On
me!—alone with me!—and I'm so sick of me! So burn!

34

—oh, burn me!—I vote for fire! (*He falls down and weeps.*)

MARCO

Well, Jason—is that your flint?

JASON (*Wryly*)

My fireball.

MARCO

Your torch. You proud to start a blaze with that?

JASON

I'd rather start with you. Say fire, Marco.

LORNA

He'd rather have you than all of us.

JASON

Yes, as a matter of fact. (*To* MARCO) If I had you, I'd give up unanimity! Say fire, Marco.

LORNA

Marco—

JASON

Stay out of this! (*To* MARCO *again*) You, Marco—you alone—!

MARCO (*On the alert*)

Why, Jason?

35

JASON
Your vote's more precious—

MARCO
I asked you why?!

JASON
If they all voted no and you said yes—enough for me!

MARCO
More precious!—why?!
(Silence, SARAH *speaks quietly.)*

SARAH
Yes. Why, Jason?

JASON *(Hotly)*
If you don't know, who does?! *(Turning back to* MARCO*)* Sooner or later, you'll be with me! Then why not sooner, while we're fresh and there's an outcry in us! Not later, Marco, through deadly deals and propositions!

MARCO
The proposition now!

JASON
Flames! . . . *(An instant. Then, quietly)* By dawn tomorrow we'll be all agreed. This way or that, unanimous. I'll start tangentially. Ignominy. Minor ignominy. One day I saw a feather on the wind. A lovely feather— every color some wild accident. It came drifting down

36

—down, down, down, down. A melody. It came to earth and fell on a rock and, in a cleft of it, got caught. It twisted. It twisted this way, that way, writhing, fluttering for whatever zephyr might lift it free. And as it quaked and quivered—out of the split in the rock there came a little head. It was a moist thing, with a mouth, mucal and lymphatic, like a rheum. Over the feather, drop by drop, it spread a yellow ooze. Then, one hair at a time, one downy hair at a time, the wet mouth ate the feather. And when the feather was all consumed, the head started to turn itself inside out. Inside out, the yellow ooze . . . the head getting smaller all the time. At last, no sign of anything. Not hair or feather, mouth or moisture . . . and the last faint track of yellow ooze dried up and blew away.

MARCO (*Dryly*)
Sad, sad. Sing dirges for a feather and an ooze.

JASON
For something! What would *you* mourn, Marco?

MARCO
Nothing's dead! All that's lived still lives!

JASON
Rejoice!

MARCO
Mourn or rejoice—is there nothing else? You live in distilled emotion, man! How can you breathe?!

37

JASON

What's your atmosphere?

MARCO

One hopes: reason.

JASON

Rarefied!

MARCO

Oh rare enough!

JASON

And you—oh, you breathe quite easily in that! But don't you dare get out of step! Close formation with the logic, boy!—matching and marching all the time! One domino after another—all those black rectangles of reason, four follows four and five follows five, until it's blank black and blank black!

MARCO

What color would you like? Don't you know the yellow daffodils are dead? The carmine is fading on the lips of the Madonna!

JASON

I didn't say Madonna!

MARCO

Prayer!

38

JASON

I didn't say prayer!

MARCO

You're always saying prayers! What color is incense?

JASON

The color of smoke!

MARCO

And where there's smoke—

JASON

Yes! What color is reason?

MARCO

It has no color, man! It never fades! It's not a lie you've told that you've got to remember! It's not abracadabra, a twelve-line sonnet!

JASON

Fourteen, by definition.

MARCO (*Quietly*)

Twelve. The sonnets are dying by decrease. The lies are eating their own tails.

JASON

Then vote for fire, Marco.

MARCO (*With a smile*)

Is it a different dying, Jason?

39

JASON (*Also smiling*)

Oh yes! And living!

MARCO

Thanks! A nice direct answer—I'll set my watch by that!

(*They all laugh a little.*)

JASON (*Airily*)

It's what you're doing all the time!

MARCO

What?—setting my watch?

JASON

Living and dying. Look at you. You're living slowly, dying rapidly! Take your temperature, my friend. You're burning up.

MARCO

To a crisp, would you think?

JASON (*Quietly, in earnest now*)

You're dying, Marco!

LORNA

No, he's not! None of us is dying!

RONALD

(*The child who has learned his lesson*)

Dying is impolite.

40

WALTER

Dying is illegal!

OTHERS

None of us is dying! None of us! None of us will ever die! We're here for always. . . . We are not going to die!—never!

SARAH (*Quietly*)

Marco does not die.

JASON (*Suddenly*)

Everybody—still! Not a sound—be still! Don't move there, Walter.

(*When all are frozen,* JASON *points to* MARCO.)

Everybody, look at him. Look closely. Watch him. He blinks his eye. He swallows. He takes a breath. His nostril quivers. He lifts his head. It's Marco. His mortality.

SARAH

Marco. His life.

JASON (*Pouncing*)

Yes! My point! Life *and* mortality! Or would you rather have only one! Which one? Walk, Marco! (*An instant.*) I said walk!

WALTER

Why should he walk if he doesn't care to?

JASON

Perhaps he'd like to tell us why he doesn't walk straight?

MARCO   (*With an easy smile*)
Don't I walk straight? I thought I did.

JASON
Walk straight, then!

LORNA
Why should he have to prove it?—he's no cripple.

SARAH
He has no infirmity.

WALTER
Infirmities are illegal.

RONALD
Infirmities are impolite.

JASON
Show them, Marco—walk!

MARCO
We're back to games again!

JASON
Do it!—walk!

SARAH
Go on, Marco. Walk straight! Show him!
(MARCO *walks across the room. Absolutely
straight, except for the last step. Pain; a gesture*

42

to his belly; he falters. A murmur of conster-
nation.)
Marco! What is it?

JASON

There!—a pain, a pain!

LORNA

Let him be!—let him alone!

OTHERS

What is it? . . . What ails him? . . . What's wrong,
Marco?

JASON

Tell them!—tell all of us!—what is it?!

MARCO

A stitch!—only a little stitch!

JASON

Where?—a stitch where?!

MARCO

In time!—saves nine!

JASON

There are only eight of us!

WALTER (*Pointing to the audience—in an ecstasy*)
There's Him!

MARCO
Shut up, you idiot! (*Another pain*) Ahh!

JASON
(*Rushing to him. A desperate plea—of rage, of pity*)
Tell me! Tell me what your pain is! Let me take it from
you!—for a moment! Let me bear it! Tell me!

MARCO (*Violently*)
Go away!

JASON
Marco—friend—brother—let me burn it out of you!

MARCO (*In a fury*)
Burn what?—what is it you really want to burn?! Sub-
stantiality? What's the bloody victory in burning that?!
Here!—you want to do it?—here's a match! Here—let's
find some kindling! Kindling!

LORNA (*Stepping forward quietly*)
Me. I'm kindling. Start with this. (*She holds the skirt
of her dress up.*)

MARCO (*Challenging* JASON)
Go on—go on!

JASON
Say fire, Marco!

44

MARCO

Me?—what do you need me for?!—go on!—light the match!

(JASON *lights the match and blows it out again. He speaks quietly to* MARCO.)

JASON

Do me an honest service, just one! I've never lied to you —don't lie to me. Suppose you had the choice?—be born or not. Come out or shrink back in the cave. Which would you choose? Well?—which? (*Pause. To the others.*) There—that's our answer. (*To* MARCO) Don't rot to corruption, Marco. Cauterize.

MARCO

Are those the only choices?

JASON

One of them is certain. You rot, Marco.

MARCO

You see that when you look at me?

JASON

I have eyes!

MARCO

Haven't you any other senses? Touch me! (*He grabs* JASON's *hand and holds it between both of his own.*) Do you feel disintegration—are you sure of that? Hear me!—do you hear me, Jason?

45

JASON

I hear your noise! You expect me to hear your silence?!

MARCO

Yes!—if you listen to me!

JASON

Why?—is there some special word I should be hearing when you never say it!

MARCO

Yes!—oh yes! (*He hurries down to speak to the audience.*) Tell me! Tell me the word! He thinks I'm bluffing! Am I? Tell me if I am! The word! What's the end of reason?—cant or incantation, which? The word!— tell me the word! Last night there was a soughing in the trees—the wind whispered sweetly. "Yes" it said. Yes and yes and yes to everything? Is that the word? Just a simple syrup, nothing more? What then? A number?—an old decrepit paradigm?—a dying arithmetic? What?! Deuteronomy? Deuteronomy and due-to-rain, no God tonight! And the darkness called He night and the evening and the morning were the first day. What of the first night?— watchman, what of the night?—the last night? Will the last be the first of anything? *What is the word?!*
(*Silence . . .* MARCO *hears nothing. He turns back to* JASON *and the others. He lies.*)
There!—did you hear it? I hope you heard it, clear as crystal—as I did.

46

JASON (*Narrowly*)

Yes. Clear as crystal. As you did. (*Then, with a cool smile*) What's the word?

MARCO

If I told you—oh man, if I just told you—you'd not believe it!

JASON

I'll try to believe it. Tell me, friend.

MARCO

Don't call me friend.

JASON

Why not?—is that the word? Is that it, my friend?

MARCO

I'm not your friend.

JASON

Ah, that's how I'll get you, friend. I'll call you friend, my friend, and get you, friend! And them—yes, all the others! Friend!—friend! (*Going quickly from one to another*)—friend! (*Then arms out, as if to embrace them all*) Family!!

OTHERS

No—we're not your family! . . . We're not related—none of us! . . . No family—not us!

47

JASON (*To* MARCO)

Shall I identify them, one by one? (*Pointing to* WALTER)
My father there!

WALTER

No.

JASON

(*Going to him, he puts his arm tightly, like a
vise, about* WALTER'S *shoulder, standing beside
him.*)
My father! Don't we look alike?

WALTER (*Struggling*)

Let go—you let me go!

JASON (*Holding fast*)

My father!—see my father!

WALTER (*Breaking away*)

I said let me go!

JASON

My father!—same eyes!—same hair!

WALTER

No!—don't listen to him!

JASON

Same sweet persuasions about God and the market place!

WALTER

No!—absolutely not!—no!

48

JASON

Let's make a litany together, Father!

WALTER

No!—somebody stop him!

JASON

I'll invoke, you supplicate—and, together, make responses! We are the Father, the Son and the Holy—

WALTER

Stop—please stop!

JASON

—Ghost! Have you ever played Ghost? It's a word game. Marco's very good at it. You must never finish a word. The man who finishes—he's so many parts of a ghost. How many parts of a ghost are you, Walter?

WALTER

I'm no part of a ghost!

JASON

What are you part of, Walter?

WALTER (*Addled*)

Nothing—I'm part of nothing!

JASON

A ghost of nothing! But you said you weren't part of a ghost.

49

WALTER
(*On the run—more and more frightened*)
I don't know—mixed up—I don't know!

JASON
You must in some way be related to a ghost, Walter!

WALTER
No—not at all—no!

JASON
Related to what, then, Walter? To me?

WALTER
No!

JASON
Am I a ghost!?

WALTER (*Frightened*)
No! I didn't say that!—no!

JASON
Then, in some way, you can be related to me, can't you,
Walter?

WALTER
Yes—I suppose so—yes.

JASON
My father!

50

WALTER

No—not your father—no!

JASON

Then you filled the questionnaire out wrong!

WALTER

I didn't fill out any questionnaire!

JASON

Then you must fill one out! Stanley—the questionnaire!
(STANLEY *steps forward and holds up an imaginary questionnaire. He writes on it with an imaginary pencil.*)

STANLEY

Your name, please.

WALTER

I'm not his father!

STANLEY

Your name!

WALTER

(*Panicked, looking to the safety of his pocket watch*)
I have no time for this!

STANLEY

No time to tell your name? Then answer any question you have time for!

WALTER

No—please—I'm overwrought!

STANLEY

When will you be underwrought?

WALTER

I'm overworked and unemployed.

STANLEY

That's very good. Are you overpopulated?

WALTER

Yes! By one!

STANLEY

Do you have a friend?

WALTER

Unto the end!

STANLEY

Are you alienated?

WALTER

Bifurcated!

STANLEY

How many numbers do you know?

WALTER

One to ten and head to toe!

52

STANLEY

Have you ever had a wife?

WALTER

Whose wife?

STANLEY

Have you ever had a child?

WALTER

Careful, there!

STANLEY

Have you ever committed sexual offenses against a ten-year-old girl?

WALTER

Eleven!

STANLEY

Eleven years old?

WALTER

No—eleven offenses.

STANLEY

Did her family mind?

WALTER

Oh no—we're old friends.

53

STANLEY

Are you well represented in all the corridors of law?

WALTER

Yes!—and in the halls of justice!

STANLEY

You're under arrest!

WALTER

You can't do that—I'll expose you!

STANLEY

As well as yourself?

WALTER

I'll expose you! I'll go to teacher and tell her you've been cheating in examination! I'll denounce you from the huskings! I'll tell the police that you're a Peeping Tom!

STANLEY

A Pooping Tim!

WALTER

And I'll tell the bishop all about you! I'll tell him that you don't keep the secrets of confessional! You betray my sacred confidence! You blabbermouth to all the other priests! You tell my sins to the altar boys and my sex life to the sexton!—you even gossip with God! I'll tell on you!—the bishop!—where the hell's the bishop?!

54

STANLEY

You're beating him!

WALTER

I do not beat the bishop!

STANLEY

You do—regularly! And I've warned you, boy, you continue in that practice and it will result in blemishes of the skin, severe acne, black nightmares, excessive perspiration, stark raving lunacy and death on a high gibbet. I say this as your friend and mother.

WALTER

You're not my friend!

STANLEY

Am I your mother?

WALTER

No!

STANLEY

Your father then!

WALTER

Stop! I know where this is leading!

STANLEY

Are you *my* father?

55

WALTER

Stop—stop short!

STANLEY

(*Pointing to* JASON) His father then?—are you his father?

(WALTER *rushes down to the audience.*)

WALTER

Stop him!—stop him short! I want to sell him short! I've had enough of this irregularity and I'm going to sell him short! Where is the Chairman of the Stock Exchange?! Where is the President of the Bourse?! I must tell you, sir, that I am shocked! I am shocked by these embezzlements, these petty peculations! To make of this glorious money marketplace a sink of improbity and theft—! I sell you short! I shorten all of you! And I warn you all that while you hang your heads in shame I will stand here with my head held high. This high, this high—I will not lower it! (*His towering indignation abates a little.*) However, I must ask you—since I will not lower my head—will someone tell me—is my fly open? . . . Never mind . . . No matter. (*Forlornly, he turns back to the others.*)

STANLEY (*Not unkindly*)

Your fly is open.

WALTER (*Sadly*)

There's been a crash.

56

STANLEY (*Commiserating*)

Yes, I know.

WALTER

The sexton knows too.

STANLEY

Yes, he told me. He told Jason too.

WALTER (*A broken man*)

Did he, Jason?

JASON (*Gently*)

Yes.

WALTER

You won't hold it against me, will you?

JASON

No, I won't.

WALTER

The police will have to be told. I've failed my re-examination. My sweetheart jilted me. The doctor's report was positive. I've not been re-elected. I've lost all my credit cards. The man in the office said I was too old. And I've broken my spectacles.

JASON

I'll buy you new ones.

WALTER

New what?

JASON

New everything.

WALTER

I wish I had a son like you.

JASON

You have.

WALTER

Am I your father then?

JASON

Yes, you are.

WALTER (*Shrewdly*)

Even if I don't vote for fire?

JASON

You will, father, you will. Sooner or later. Just rest.

WALTER

You're very kind to me. Things have to seem more beautiful than they really are, or we'll perish. Don't you think so, Jason?

JASON

Just rest, father.

58

WALTER

Yes. I'm an old man. All I want is a chocolate, a smile and my afternoon nap.

JASON

Sit here. (*He gently seats* WALTER.)

WALTER

Thank you, son.
                    (MARCO *applauds grimly*.)

MARCO

Beautiful! How beautifully you got him.

JASON

I didn't get him. He begot himself.

DELIA

What's wrong with being gotten? I wouldn't mind being gotten by Jason.

JASON

Thank you, Delia.

DELIA

Get me, Jason.

JASON

Another relative. (*Introducing* DELIA) My sister.

DELIA

No—not your sister!

JASON

I said sister.

DELIA

No—I don't want that!

STANLEY

Don't be shortsighted, duck. Sister or no sister, all things are possible.

DELIA

I will not be his sister, no! I was hoping for better than that!

STANLEY (*Conspiratorially*)

Take sister for a start, idiot. Take it and develop it, develop it!

DELIA

Really . . . ?

STANLEY

Go on—go on!

DELIA

I—how do I look?

STANLEY

Quite lovely, darling, let me warm you up for him. (*He takes* DELIA *in his arms. His hand caresses her back and her buttocks.*) You're really delicious, you know, now that you've aged a little. Most meat is at its best when it starts to rot.

60

(DELIA *giggles.*)

JASON

Stay out of it, Stanley, if it's all the same to you.

STANLEY

Everything's all the same to me. (*He starts rolling his pelvis against* DELIA's.) How's that, dearie, you like it?
(*As she giggles delightedly*)
Motor revving up a little, is it? Good. (*Gently pushing her away*) Now you go on, go bang your brother, darling, there's a good girl.

DELIA   (*Siding seductively to* JASON)

Brother . . . will you dance with me?

JASON   (*With a wry smile*)

Yes, but I warn you, when a man dances with his sister, it's not classic for him to run amuck.
(*She looks to* STANLEY. *He winks and advises, confidentially.*)

STANLEY

Take your chances!

DELIA   (*To* JASON)

I'll take my chances!
(*She throws herself into* JASON's *arms and they start to dance.*)
Sing!—somebody, sing!

61

STANLEY (*Singing*)

As I was walking in the bois,
I chanced upon a fille de joie—

DELIA

Louder—faster, Stanley! Somebody, beat something!
Ronald, beat a drum!
(RONALD *beats a small spade on a toy sand pail.*
He blows a whistle. He rings toy bells. STANLEY
claps his hands as he sings, WALTER *joins him.*)
You sing fast and we'll dance slow! Hold me tighter,
Jason—please!—tighter! Louder, everybody!—louder!
Can't you hold me tighter? No—let me go! Let me go
—I can't breathe—let me go! Oh, let me go!
(*She breaks away. Silence. Everybody watches*
her. JASON *is motionless, with a still smile on his*
face.)

JASON

What's the matter, sister?

DELIA

I—my breath—I—(*She tries to laugh.*) It got so warm
—I couldn't catch my breath—isn't anybody warm?
Aren't you warm, Lorna?

LORNA

Just warm enough to be alive.

DELIA

No—*warm* warm! If it weren't indelicate—considering

62

the proposition—I'd say hot! Yes, hot—I *will* say it—
hot! Will anyone mind if I wear less clothing?

STANLEY

Take something off, love.

DELIA

Yes, I will—I will! (*In full view, she reaches up under
her skirt and pulls her panties off.*) Oh, what a relief!
Oh happy day, what a relief! (*Waving her panties*) My
banner of freedom! (*She kicks, she bends, she does
pushups, she runs about the room.*) Who wants my
panties?—does anyone want my panties? Jason—Walter
—Ronald, would you like my panties?

RONALD

No, thank you—I have my own.

DELIA

Stanley, would you like my panties?

STANLEY

It was on the tip of my tongue to ask.

DELIA

They're yours—they're yours, Stanley.

STANLEY
(*With studied dignity and decorum*)

I will keep them always. I will cherish them as a memento
of this glorious occasion. (*Saying which, he spreads the
elastic and slips the panties onto his head, as a cap. Everybody laughs.*

DELIA *is humiliated. She reaches for the panties. He fends her off. She starts to strike at him.*)

DELIA

Give them back! You dirty miserable degenerate—give them back! Give me my pants!—give me—give me!
(*They are fighting. She is struggling with him and he is biting her, tearing her hair. They are both screaming.*)

JASON (*Rushing in to separate them*)
Stop it—stop it, both of you!

DELIA

Oh, Jason—Jason!—thank heaven you came along! There I was on this dark street and out of the alleyway! —this depravity!—he attacked me from the alleyway! Oh, hold me!

JASON (*Holding her off*)
Stand off, sister.

DELIA

Hold me—I'm burning up—put your hand on my breast! —hold my breast!—hold me!

JASON

Stand off, I say!

DELIA

I'm burning! Fire! I vote for you, Jason! I vote for fire!
(*Dead stillness. Nobody stirs. Very gently* JASON *takes a misplaced lock of* DELIA'S *hair*

64

and lays it back where it belongs. He straight-
ens the shoulder of her dress. Silently. The look
on her face is deathly frightened. She is horri-
fied at what she has said.)

JASON (*Quietly. Even a little sadly*)
Another vote. There are now three of us.
(STANLEY *and* DELIA *are close to* JASON.)

RONALD (*Quietly*)
I want to go home.

JASON
You are home, Ronald.

RONALD
No, I'm not.

JASON (*To* MARCO, *while pointing to* RONALD)
You know what *he* is to me?

MARCO
Your son?

JASON
How did you guess? My son. (*To* RONALD) And this
is your home.

RONALD (*With firm certainty*)
No it's not. I would recognize it if it were. I'd know it
by the curtains and the dog. You see this lead?—it always
had a dog on it. There's no dog here. And no smell of

65

one. My dog smells of rain. When I come in from out-doors, I know he's there—the scent of him. If there were a puppy here that I could put on this lead, I might be fooled into thinking . . . well . . . imagining. But not for long. I'd know it soon enough, that I'm not home. . . . You're not my father.

JASON

You're home, Ronald.

RONALD

No!—no I'm not! (*He hurries down to the footlights.*) He lies to me! Why do you let him do that!? Why don't you come for me? If you're too busy, send for me! Send someone! Send my father, send my mother, send the cook! Or the dog! Oh yes—please send the dog! Or send a telegram! "Please send Ronald back! Ronald is needed at home!" Couldn't you send a telegram? I swear that I will destroy nothing! I will just play with my toys, I will draw pigs with crayons and I will throw away all the noisy tin whistles! I will not light matches—I will never light a match again! Oh please—oh send for me! (*He hurries back to the others. Without a word, he starts to gather up all his toys, very busily.*)

JASON

What are you doing, Ronald? (*Silence.*) Ronald, what are you doing?

RONALD

They're sending for me.

66

JASON

Who, Ronald?

RONALD

They said I was to gather up my things.

JASON

Whom are they sending, Ronald?

RONALD

They'll be here any minute—I mustn't keep him waiting.

JASON

Keep whom waiting, Ronald?

RONALD

Him.

JASON

Who, Ronald?

RONALD

My brother.

JASON

You haven't got a brother, Ronald.

RONALD *(Nettled, disturbed)*

My . . . my . . .

JASON

Who?

RONALD

My dog! They're sending my dog. He's taking me home!

JASON

You are home, Ronald.

RONALD

No.

JASON (*Taking his toys from him*)

Yes, Ronald. . . . Ask Marco.

RONALD (*Slowly turning to* MARCO)

Am I home? (*Silence.*) Marco, I will believe you if you say it. Am I home?

JASON

He said he will believe you.

RONALD

Am I home?

(*Silence. In wild terror,* RONALD *starts to flee. There is no place to go. He stops. He lets out a bloody cry, streaks across the stage and falls into* SARAH's *lap, sobbing convulsively.*)

MARCO

You're quite a monster, Jason.

(LORNA *laughs quietly.*)

JASON

Which one do you laugh at?—him or me?

(LORNA *laughs again.* JASON *introduces her. His
smile is ironic.*)
My beloved. My wife. My mistress. The doxy of my
heart.

MARCO

Yes. This one I believe—no blood relationship.

JASON

You make too much of blood. There are other juices.
Sperm and spittle. Some say they're much the same.

MARCO

Which is it between you two?

JASON

Both. Which between *you* two?

MARCO

Spit. All spittle.

LORNA (*With a smile*)

The other also.

MARCO (*Quietly*)

She lies.

LORNA

Of course. To both of you. Which do I love? Who has
the key to my bawdyhouse? Which of you is in my bed?
—and which is under it? Go on, find out—kill each
other.

69

MARCO

Charming, isn't she? Your wife, you say? Her soul's a soiled rag.

JASON (*Smiling*)

Still . . . she's the best, I'll bet. (*Touching her clothes as if she were inanimate*) Under all this filthy flapdoodle —under all this dismal dinge and disorder—she's the best. The silly romantic best.

DELIA

After me, she'll be the first to vote for fire.

JASON (*Studiously*)

Yes . . . I think so.
          (LORNA *laughs quietly.*)
You laugh a lot.

LORNA

What made you notice?

JASON

She laughs even while we're making love. She thinks climax is a joke.

MARCO

Or a fable?

LORNA

Yes, a fable.

70

JASON

She laughs a lot, she lies a lot. No fable. She loves me.

(LORNA *laughs again.*)

She's in love with—splendor! She thinks she has a choice. But no—not really. Just two ways of saying the same thing: To go up in flames—or down in flames. (*To* LORNA) They're both the same, my dear. And when you go—you'll flame in all directions. (*Again touching her dress*) It's flimsy, this material. It's made of dreams. (*Suddenly, he grabs her in an embrace.*)

LORNA

Hands off!—stop it! Let me go!

JASON (*Enraged*)

Deny you love me! Go on, deny it! Deny you love finality—the end of muck and maybes and subjunctives! The flaming finish . . . that's what you want! The blaze across the sky! deny it: you're in love with fire as I am and—by axiom, by postulate, things equal to the same— you love me!

(*She is contemptuously silent. He lets her go. Keeping his eye on her lest she move a muscle,* JASON *backs away from her and points to where he knows* MARCO *is.*)

Whom do you love?—not him! Why, lady, he's perishing with cold! His life is freezing inside an icy cerebellum! Not him?!

(*Another silence.* JASON *turns and faces* MARCO *with a little mocking laugh.*)

You know . . . I think she loves us both. Good. I'll share you with her—and her with you.

71

Thanks. No need. She's yours.

Mine how? Secondhand? You've had her. How many times? Once—twice—a hundred?

If it depends on number, ten cows can catch one butterfly. I've had her—never!

You're lying! Lorna—has he?

(*With a wry laugh*)
The answer's yes and no. A little and a lot. If and possibly. How would you like a small perhaps? How would you like a kick in the ass?

Marco, the truth!

When will you believe me? I'm alone. Ask anyone. I'm everybody's stranger. I haven't touched her. No—nor anyone. Measure the distance between me and everybody else! I'm alone!

I don't believe it!

MARCO

Alone! And so are you!

JASON

Not true!

MARCO

We're none of us related!

JASON

No! Not true!

MARCO

(*Seeing* JASON's *alarm: suddenly gentle*)
Jason—please—don't let it frighten you! It's not as bad
—believe me—not nearly so terrifying as it sounds!
We've been a long time coming to this place!—a long
time, Jason! It's something that we've won!—in bloody
battle!—won! Do you remember love? the killing love?
—the kiss that suffocates?—the garroting embrace? Do
you remember—oh, the insufficiencies of air! (*As if
strangling for breath*) Air, Jason—take a breath! Breathe,
Jason! Air!
(JASON *is still. He studies* MARCO *carefully.*)

JASON

I wonder . . . are you truly alone? . . . all that im-
maculate?

MARCO

There's no one, Jason.

73

JASON

There's me.

MARCO

Jason—

JASON

You're dear to me, Marco—

MARCO

A nuisance to you, yes!

JASON

My closest relative!

MARCO

We're not related—not at all!

JASON

Let's talk of consanguinity!

MARCO

Blood again, is it?

JASON

Oh yes, the richest kind—type one to type infinity—
bad blood!

MARCO

Bad blood, yes!

74

My enemy!

MARCO (*Triumphant*)
All right!—that blood I *will* admit! Your enemy! Your
dearest relative! I'm the one you need the most because
I'll stop you! All right, then, down you go! (*Taking
over—to the others—stampeding the meeting*) The meeting's over! Get up! Delia—up! Walter—move! The
meeting's over! Everybody—out! No flames today! The
fire has been called because of rain! No fire—the meeting's over! Your belongings—take them! Toys!—panta-
loons!—your hat! The meeting's over!
> (*The meeting starts breaking up. Noise. Laugh-
> ter. Relief. Gibes at* JASON. *Kisses of departure.
> Pandemonium. Only* SARAH *remains seated, knit-
> ting quietly.*)

JASON
No—stop! All of you—stop! Sit down! Wait!
> (*He reaches into* RONALD'S *bag of toys and pulls
> out a watchman's rattle. He makes a din with
> it. No one pays attention. Then:*)
The trial!—come back!—the trial!
> (*As they hear him say "trial" they stop. Slowly
> they turn. They look at one another. They are
> tensely still. Even* MARCO.)

WALTER (*Quietly, hopefully*)
Will there really be a trial?

75

MARCO

Oh yes, a mock trial, you can be sure of that! (*To* JASON) And we've had plenty of those!

JASON

What, boy, you want a real one?—with robes and justice? Well, there might be, you know!—and you not here to testify! Want to miss it, Marco?
(*Silence.* MARCO *takes a step back into the group.*)
No, I didn't think so. Come now, meet another member of my family.

MARCO

Another enemy?

JASON

Family, I said—a friend's an enemy—a little love, a little loathing.

MARCO

Who?

JASON

My mother.

MARCO

You never had a mother, Jason! Where?

JASON

There!
(*He points to* SARAH. MARCO *slowly turns to*

76

look at her. Just as slowly SARAH *raises her head from her knitting. An instant of tense silence.*)

MARCO (*Almost gently*)
She's not your mother, Jason.

JASON (*To lead him across the room*)
Come.

MARCO (*Quietly—pleading*)
Jason, don't! She's a killer. She'll kill one of us. You, perhaps. She'll turn your bones soft, she'll suck the breath out of you. (*But he is allowing himself to be led across the room.*)

JASON
(*Introducing, with dignity and pride*)
My mother, Marco.

MARCO (*Pleading*)
Sarah—tell him—he's not your son. He's a strong man —he has no need of anyone—tell him that. Tell him he's not your son.

SARAH (*Turning gently to* JASON)
You're not my son. (*Pointing to* MARCO) *He* is.
(*The others laugh.*)

MARCO (*An outcry*)
No! Goddamn you, no!

77

SARAH (*Quietly*)

Yes. You are my son.

(*Pause.* MARCO *pulls himself under control. He turns to* JASON.)

MARCO

Did you hear that idiocy?

JASON

It didn't strike me idiotic. I knew someone must be tied to you and you to someone. Why not a mother?—why not Sarah?

MARCO

Yes—why not Sarah? Better to have Sarah for a mother than—let's say—Stanley.

STANLEY

Me be your mother?—would you consider it?—how dear of you!

(MARCO *hurries back to* SARAH'S *side. He entreats her with desperation.*)

MARCO

Sarah, tell him: enough of this! You and I—we have the best relationship that ever was—we're strangers! (*In a sudden rage*) Talk! Tell them I'm not your son! You made me up—out of wet eyes and dry dreams and frenzied estrogen!

SARAH

Gently, son.

78

MARCO

I'm not your son!

SARAH

What is your pain, Marco?

MARCO

I've eaten too much moon!—green cheese does not agree
with me!

SARAH

What is it, Marco?

MARCO

Nothing!

SARAH

A while ago—when you walked from there to there
. . . What was the pain?

MARCO

Which one would you like?—I have a large variety! If
I drink too much, I sweat. If I eat an extra sweet, I fart!
Shall I do a small convulsion?

SARAH

What hurts you, Marco?

MARCO (*His rage growing*)

Will you stop that mother-talk?

79

JASON

Let her comfort you!

MARCO

Get her away from me!

JASON

She's your mother!

MARCO

No! (*He grabs her.*) Look, everybody—look at us to-gether!—look at us!

SARAH (*Struggling to get away*)

Marco, let me go!

MARCO (*Not releasing her*)

Look at us! Be fair! Judge us! Could she be my mother? Is there one feature of resemblance between us?

JASON *and* SARAH (*Together*)

Let her go! . . . Marco, please!

MARCO (*Riding through them*)

Her eyes!—look at her eyes!—look at mine! her mouth! Her face—feature by feature! Do we walk, do we talk the same? If there's a relationship—my sister! Perhaps my wife! (*Abruptly he changes his tight grasp of her and holds her off at arm's length.*) Are you?—are you my wife?!

80

JASON *and* **SARAH**

Marco, stop it! . . . Let me go—oh please let me go!

MARCO

Are you my wife? Do you want a son? Do you want a son of *me?* Here—right now—right here—so it can be witnessed—

SARAH

Let me go!

MARCO

—witnessed as yours!—witnessed as mine! Make room —all of you—make room—right here—right now!
(*He starts to throw* SARAH *down on the floor, himself on top of her.*)

OTHERS (*Rushing toward them*)

Stop him! . . . Stop it! . . . Let her alone! . . . For shame, for shame to your mother! . . . Go on, Marco —don't let them stop you! . . . No—no—no!!
(*They pull* MARCO *and* SARAH *apart. The men hold* MARCO.)

WALTER

Shameful—how shameful! What an abomination to treat your mother this way!

MARCO

You treat her that way, then! Go at her! Impregnate her! Someone!

81

WALTER

We should drive him out!

DELIA

We should burn him out!

JASON

Let him go!

WALTER

Let him go?—certainly not!

JASON

I said let him go!

STANLEY

No! The frolic's just beginning!

JASON

Stanley—

STANLEY

No! We can get a mile-high high-jinks out of him!

JASON

Hands off, I said!

STANLEY

The hell with you!
(JASON *smashes* STANLEY *across the face.* STAN-
LEY *lets* MARCO *go and confronts* JASON.)

82

Do it again!

(JASON *hits him again.*)

Once again—again!

(*As* JASON *hits him again and again,* STANLEY *cries out.*)

Oh, harder—smash me—hit me, Jason—oh, please hit me —again, oh once again! (*Now on his knees and bleeding,* STANLEY *weeps.*) Oh, thank you, Jason—thank you, love—Jason, thank you! (*He grabs* JASON's *hands and kisses each one, then kisses* JASON's *trouser legs, his shoes, crying out, sobbing.*)

WALTER (*In revulsion at* STANLEY's *display*)

Stop that! Stop that, it's disgusting! Why doesn't somebody stop him?!

SARAH (*Going to* STANLEY)

Why didn't somebody stop *him*? (*She indicates* JASON.)

WALTER

Stop both of them! Who's in charge here? Isn't anyone in charge? (*Silence. Deflated again*) Nobody? Oh murder, I can remember when someone was in charge. There were gods and kings in those days. And bright parades and rituals. The human mystery was beautiful and we didn't poke at it! (*Angry*) Now we turn it inside out and dig at its bloody entrails! And there's no place to hide! We're out here—exposed to one another—catching our death! (*Forlorn again*) Isn't anyone in charge?

83

SARAH

(*Handing her handkerchief to* STANLEY)

Here, you're bleeding. (*Then, wryly*) How like my son
you are!

MARCO

If you mean me—oh yes, I see the resemblance! It's very
clear!

SARAH

You think not?—just look at him: enjoying it.

MARCO

If you mean pain, I have no appetite for it!

SARAH

You don't? You raven for it.

MARCO

You mean I'm that!? (*And he points to* STANLEY.)

SARAH

One way or another. Greedy. Keep it all to yourself.
(*To the others*) When he was born, I didn't feel a
twinge. Not a single pang. No matter what the ladies
say, there's only so much pain in childbirth—and he took
all of it. I used to think: he's hoarding pain. But I think
differently now. I think he's sharing it with someone.

JASON

With whom?

84

I wish I knew. (*To* MARCO) I wish you'd share it with me.

MARCO (*With a smile*)
Why?—you want to deliver me to my enemy? (*And he points to* JASON.)

SARAH (*Pointing to* MARCO *himself*)
From, Marco—from your enemy! What's your pain?
(*Silence.* MARCO *looks at her, then at* JASON. *He surveys the entire room. He gets a shrewd look in his eyes.*)

MARCO
Yes . . . I think I'll tell you. Why not? I'll tell you.
(*Tense silence.*)
. . . I have a rat in my stomach.
(*The silence holds. He looks from one to another again. Then he laughs.* STANLEY *is the first to believe his laugh. He joins in the laughter.*)

STANLEY
A rat!—that's lovely!

MARCO (*Quickly*)
Yes—isn't it?

STANLEY (*Laughing harder*)
Oh, sublime! Did you hear him?—Delia, did you hear him?

(DELIA *starts to laugh.*)

Lovely, right? Scratch a poet, find a clown! A rat in his stomach!

> (RONALD, *not quite comprehending, laughs because the others do. Soon everyone is laughing with the exception of* SARAH. MARCO *laughs loudest.*)

OTHERS

Rat in his stomach! . . . Did you hear that? . . . That's told her, hasn't it? . . . Told us all, didn't he? . . . Rat in his stomach!

> (*The laughter mounts and diminishes. As it fades, everyone disappears, in darkness. All except* MARCO. *He stands in a pinpoint of light and speaks to the audience:*)

MARCO

Rat in my stomach . . . I told them—just as you said I should. And they laughed—just as you said they would. I'd have told them sooner if I'd thought they wouldn't believe me. But you were right—they did laugh. Laughter: a glimpse of the world-out-of-kilter—and knowing that's the kilter of it! Well, they thought *I* made the joke. I'd gladly give *you* proper credit for it if I knew how to introduce you. You wouldn't care to tell me, would you? No, I thought not. Well, thanks for the joke anyway. I've precious else to thank you for. Oh, I could thank you for the rat. At least you've given me *something* that hurts. It's better than having nothing— and have *that* hurt. A blessing, really. Oh, a minor blessing. A devil's blessing, shall we say? Devil—what

86

an old-fashioned word! Tell me, is *that* what you are? Oh, I'd give you anything to have a good old-fashioned devil!—come, come, don't hide any more! Show me your face. If I had a picture of you—would it be a devil's face? . . . Would it be the face of a rat?
 (*The circle of light widens and we see* LORNA
 has been listening.)

LORNA
Did you get any response?

MARCO
Hundreds of them. Antiphonal, all echoes. (*Calling*) Hello—hello! Anybody home?—anybody home? . . . Did I say echo? Ecco means behold.

LORNA
Don't pun. (*As he grimaces—a stab of pain*) Where does it ache?

MARCO (*Pointing up*)
Out there, I think. No—there! (*Quietly, to* LORNA) Go away.

LORNA
Have you tried everything?

MARCO
Oh yes. Camomile tea. Angels and aspirin. Rutting, in season. A dose of mathematics.

LORNA

A hard heroic dose?

MARCO

No, an easy one. As easy as falling off a logarithm.

LORNA

Is there a mathematical correlation between a man's pain and the puns he inflicts?

MARCO

You have come to the right authority—I am the Pundit of Pain!

LORNA (*In a sudden outburst of anger*)

Stop it!

MARCO (*A flare of rage*)

Pain is the lowest form of humor! (*Silence. When he speaks again he is still enraged, but he doesn't raise his voice.*) Why did you tell them about us?

LORNA (*Quickly*)

I didn't!

MARCO

Oh, they guessed! Jason and Sarah—they both guessed!

LORNA

Is it so hard to guess?

MARCO

You told them! When Jason asked, you didn't say no, you said: "A little and a lot." You miserable tart, why didn't you tell him no?!

LORNA

You told him no—did he believe you? We don't believe the answers any more! We use them to find the questions!

MARCO

Find the questions!

LORNA

They won't find me! If they really look at me by daylight, they'll see how ugly I am!

MARCO

Don't!

LORNA

Ugly!—and no one ever sees me nighttime! (*A moment. Then, quietly*) Only you, Marco . . . when you make love to me. . . . Will you ever by daylight?

MARCO

No.

LORNA

I think you will. You have a rat, you say? I think you will. (*Moving closer to him*) Stand straight. Let me see how tall you are. Come close.

MARCO

Nighttime, yes!

LORNA

Now!

MARCO

Nighttime, when we're both beautiful! (*Pointing to her broken tiara*) When this bottle glass is emerald! Moonlight, when my palms are dry and you're not—

LORNA

—an old hag!

MARCO

I didn't say that!

LORNA

Young hag! All hags are young these days! Nobody's old anymore! We all live longer and die sooner. One day we'll be born old and live dead. We'll conceive ourselves coming and going. Come to me—love me by daylight.

MARCO

No! Daytime I have to see what's there—which way to run!

LORNA

Where are you safe?

MARCO

Behind words!

90

LORNA

They're your prison—come out!

MARCO

Wait!—do something for me—tell Jason I've gone!

LORNA

Gone?

MARCO

Gone!—bellamirado! Gone up in a puff of smoke!—tell
him that!

LORNA

No!

MARCO (*Turning on her*)

No puff of smoke?—why not? Didn't he send you to
smoke me out?

LORNA

No!

MARCO (*Enraged*)

He sent you!—admit it!
                    (*He grabs her.*)

LORNA (*Struggling to get away*)

No!

MARCO

Admit it!—sent you after me!

LORNA

No!—let me go, let me go! (*Breaking away. With an outcry*) I'll get you, you murderer!

MARCO

Get me and what'll you have?!

LORNA (*Wild*)

I'll get you—some day—midmorning—I'll get you! With aphrodisiacs!

MARCO (*He laughs.*)

Ah, lovely!—dragon milk?

LORNA

Yes!

MARCO

In a small vial?

LORNA

A vial of rage! And an oleander leaf to chew on!

MARCO

Is it really mortal? I hear it's poisonous!

LORNA

Yes, if you eat it, it dies!

MARCO

Good! I'll eat it and kiss you!

92

LORNA

And the best aphrodisiac of all!

MARCO

Oh, please—the best! Fire?!

LORNA

You think I would?!

MARCO

Yes!

LORNA

You bastard, you'll come to love me one night and I'll
piss on you!

MARCO *(Quietly)*

Go away!

LORNA

You come looking for my beautiful bright eyes in the
dark and I'll drive you out to suck your own semen!

MARCO *(Wearily)*

Well said.
    (Silence. She is suddenly filled with self-revul-)
    sion)

LORNA

How ugly I am!

93

MARCO (*Quietly, with deep commiseration*)
No, Lorna . . . don't.

LORNA

Ugly—

MARCO (*Gently*)
Lorna!

LORNA

—trying to dress up my sores—

MARCO

Please! Don't say that!

LORNA

—*diseased!*

MARCO

Lorna—please!

LORNA (*Weeping*)
Why do you come to me at night and say I'm beautiful?

MARCO

Because you are.

LORNA

Why don't you say ugly—say it!

94

MARCO

(*A moment. He holds her. He speaks quietly, gently.*)
Do you really want me to?

LORNA (*Sobbing softly*)
No. If you were to say it—oh, I think my blood would
turn gray! But if you love me—!

MARCO
You make too much of love.

LORNA
Can too much be made of it?

MARCO
Oh yes, in the darkness. Riddle: Why do lovers love the
dark? So they can lie in it.

LORNA
I wish you'd kiss me and say I love you.

MARCO
In all this bloody glare?—say "love"?

LORNA
It's only a short lie but it goes a long distance.

MARCO
Wouldn't it go further if it were the truth?

95

LORNA

Love doesn't have to be the truth. Only a little alibi. Hell knows we need it.

MARCO

Oh, if I could make love and find the truth, I'd kiss a cobra!

LORNA

Perhaps you can't have both!

MARCO

Why not? I can rub my belly and pat my head! (*He does it.*) You see? I'm blessed with talent!

LORNA

Please kiss me.

MARCO

Yes!—find the truth! (*He kisses her.*)

LORNA

What did you find?

MARCO

A dear, dear, precious . . . lie.

LORNA

But precious you said! Oh love, we've tried so many things!—let's try plain kindness!

96

MARCO (*Gently*)

Yes, we'll sing old songs and tell each other sweet old fairy tales.

LORNA

Oh yes—please!—tell me one!

MARCO

I can't think of one that has no monster in it. (*His pain again*) Ah!

LORNA

Oh, let me help you!

MARCO

No!

LORNA

Let me share the pain with you!

MARCO

No, it's my own, it's what I'm sure of!
     (JASON *has appeared. Watching them, he speaks quietly.*)

JASON

Is it all you're sure of?

MARCO

So he did send you, after all!

97

LORNA

No—he wants you to think he did!

MARCO

It's what I think, all right!

JASON

Oh yes, watch her, Marco—she's devious. (*To* LORNA) And you watch him! He says night and he means day. He says beautiful and he means ugly! . . . What does he mean when he says rat?

MARCO (*Quickly*)

He means something to laugh at!

JASON

Oh yes. And laugh we did. Until our bellies hurt. . . . How's yours?

MARCO

My what?

JASON

Your belly. (*Very quiet*) Go get the others, Lorna.
    (*Silence. She looks from one to the other of them.*)
I said get the others! Fetch!
    (*Now she looks only at* MARCO. *He turns away. She departs.*)
Twice now I've heard the thing discussed today.
        (*As* MARCO *turns to go*)
No—don't go. Twice. Three's a mystic number. Let's mention it again.

98

MARCO

Mention what?

JASON

Your rat.

MARCO

It was a joke!

JASON

Let's pretend it's serious. Is it a real one, with a tail?
Brown or gray variety? Or many colors, like a feather
I used to know. Is it silent?—does it sing? A rat can sing,
you know. What's the melody?

MARCO

Mine is silent. How's yours?

JASON (*Gently*)

In your gut, did you say? Your gut?

MARCO

No! Nowhere!

JASON

Where is it, man? Your head?—your kidneys?—on your
back?

MARCO

None!—there isn't any!

JASON

You reached for your belly! That's a surprise! I'd have thought: your head! But gut? You, Marco?—you disappoint me!

(*As* MARCO *makes to leave again*)

I said don't go! Don't worry about it, boy—an ancient use for fire!

MARCO (*Alert*)

What?

JASON

Burn out the rats!

MARCO (*With a wary smile*)

Oh no! I won't vote for it, Jason!

JASON

When I show you the efficacy of a very small flame—

MARCO

Candleflame!

JASON

Just bright enough to read by!

MARCO

Thank you—that's all I ever want!

JASON

You fool!—you're trapped in your own luggage!

MARCO

Hands off!

JASON

You hurt and you're hungry!

MARCO (*Ironically*)

Hungry?—not me!—I can make a meal on a communion
wafer!

JASON

What's left for you in this place? A door with a lock on
it and no key? Another spoon of gruel, another crust of
bread? A picture on a wall that cries illusion, illusion?!
A thought? Is there one thought you've ever had that
hasn't betrayed you? Is there one word that has ever held
still long enough for you to embrace it? What are you
in love with? *Your rat?!*
  (*A long silence. The thought strikes* JASON
  powerfully.)
Oh murder, that's it, isn't it?—in love with your own
pain!

MARCO

No! I loathe it!

JASON

Good! I'll rid you of it!
  (*The others start coming in quickly.*)

MARCO

No!

JASON

(*To the others. He points to the chest of drawers.*)
Stanley—Walter—move that thing—and him onto it!

MARCO

No! (*He starts to run.*)

JASON

Don't let him get away!
(*The men seize* MARCO.)

MARCO

No—let me go—let me go!

VOICES

Hold him! Don't let him get away! Up here—up here!

JASON

He has a rat inside him! Hold! Hold him!

LORNA

No—let him go!

SARAH

Please—let him go!

JASON

You want him to die of pain?!

VOICES

Now, Jason!—do it now! Hold him! Don't move!—lie
still, lie still!

102

JASON

Lights! Strike out the lights!

VOICES

Lights!—the lights!
(*The lights go out. In the darkness a taper is
lighted. It flickers fitfully in the dark.*)

MARCO

Oh please—oh please—

JASON (*In a violent outcry*)

Bring me something! Bring me something that's alive!
Something with blood on it!

VOICES

Now, Jason!—now!

MARCO

No—no!

JASON

Give me that flame! Now hold him! Hold still, my
friend! Hold still, my love! Hold still, my enemy!
(MARCO *writhes on the chest of drawers. The
light gutters over him. It is as though he's on
an operating table, with the surgeons all about
him. Now, a scream from one of the women,
a sob from someone, a muffled outcry.* JASON
holds it up—a bloody rat.)

JASON (*As if to a lover*)

You're freed of it, my friend! You're free!

ACT TWO

From twilight to night. RONALD *appears. He calls off-stage, to a dog.*

RONALD

Come on! Come on, boy—come on, that's a good dog! I said come on! (*He puts his fingers in his mouth and whistles a shrill blast.*) Come on, you fool dog, don't sniff around one hydrant all day!—there's a whole world of hydrants to discover! Well, boy, I'm going to have to put you on a lead, willy-nilly, that's what I'm going to do!

> (*He takes the lead out of his pocket and goes offstage with it. A moment and he returns, pulling the recalcitrant dog behind him. The dog is* STANLEY, *on all fours.*)

There now, if you're a bad dog and don't mind your manners, on the lead you go! But if you're good and come to heel, somebody rubs your neck and scratches your ears and feeds you a biscuit.

> (STANLEY *sits up on his hind legs, pants, lets his tongue wag and tries to ingratiate himself.*)

How disgusting you are! At the first sound of the word biscuit you're ready to lick my hand!

(STANLEY *licks* RONALD's *hand.* RONALD *giggles.*)
Stop that!—oh, stop that!—oh please, oh stop!
           (STANLEY *stops licking him.*)
No, no, I didn't mean for you *really* to stop! I mean I
like it so much I can't stand it! (*Giggling and laughing*)
Do it again!
           (*As* STANLEY *starts to lick him again.*)
No, no—stop!
           (*As* STANLEY *stops,* RONALD *has a flare of rage.*)
Damn you, why did you stop?!
           (STANLEY *skulks as far away as his leash will*
           allow him. He buries his head in his forepaws.
           He sulks.)
I'm sorry.
           (*No response from* STANLEY)
I said I'm sorry. I'm sorry, doggie, I really am. You want
a biscuit?

      STANLEY (*Jumping up ecstatically*)
Yes, I do!

RONALD
Don't talk! Frisk!—frisk about!—if you want to show
me how happy you are, frisk, frisk!
           (STANLEY *frisks about.* RONALD *tosses him a*
           biscuit—beyond the reach of the leash. STAN-
           LEY *rushes to catch it and gets snapped back by*
           the shortness of the leash.)

STANLEY
You son of a bitch, you threw that thing beyond the
reach of the lead!

106

RONALD

Don't talk!

STANLEY

What the hell you trying to do?—strangle me?

RONALD

I said don't talk! You want to be a dog, you say woof
or bow-wow or rarf!

STANLEY

I'll talk, I'll talk!

RONALD

All right then, it's over!

STANLEY

Rarf! . . . Rarf—rarf!

RONALD

That's better. Now, lie down. Roll over and I'll pat you.
I'll give you another biscuit and I'll tickle your belly.
Come along!

> (STANLEY *returns to* RONALD. *He lets himself be
> patted, rubbed, scratched. He turns over on his
> back and* RONALD *rubs his belly as* STANLEY *lets
> out moans of delight.*)

There!—see what happens to a good doggie? If I'm going too far, you let me know and I'll stop.

STANLEY

No—don't.

RONALD *(Warning)*

Rarf.

STANLEY

Rarf!

RONALD

Been keeping your teeth clean?—let me see your teeth.
(*He pushes* STANLEY's *lips back and explores his
teeth, his tongue, his gums.*) Doggie wants a rubber
bone to chew on—keep his teeth clean, make his
gums nice and strong!

STANLEY

Ow!—you're hurting me!

RONALD

Rarf!

STANLEY

No, dammit—let my mouth alone!
(*As* RONALD *makes another reach for* STANLEY's
mouth, the latter grabs RONALD's *fingers in his
teeth and hangs on.*)

RONALD

Ow! Let go! Let go, let go!
(STANLEY *hangs on and* RONALD *pummels him.
They fight, they roll about,* STANLEY's *teeth
still clamped on* RONALD's *fingers.* RONALD *is
screaming with pain. At last he breaks away.*)

108

You bastard!—you mean miserable bastard!—look at my hand!—look!—it's bleeding!

STANLEY

Serves you damn right!

RONALD

Rarf!

STANLEY

Rarf yourself, you little worm!

RONALD

I didn't ask you to be my dog!—you begged me!

STANLEY

You begged me to beg you!

RONALD

You agreed! You agreed to be my dog!

STANLEY

That was *my* side of the bargain!

RONALD

There wasn't any *my* side *to* the bargain! I didn't have to do anything but pat you from time to time and scratch your neck!

STANLEY

Oh, come now!

RONALD

What else?
> (STANLEY *simpers*. RONALD *starts to get a little
> alarmed, a little embarrassed. He draws his coat
> collar closer across his breast.*)

What else?!

STANLEY

(*The simper slowly disappears. He is sober-faced now.*)
Come on.

RONALD (*Apprehensive*)

Where?

STANLEY

I said come on.

RONALD (*With bravado*)

If you think you're going to spread-eagle me somewhere
across a rock—!
> (STANLEY *smiles quietly, without mirth. There
> is a forlorn dignity about him as he speaks.*)

STANLEY

No. I've been across a rock with prettier things than you.
Long ago. Oh, those were beguiling times, they were!
Every spring rain was sent to me—*personally!* And
everything I did—no matter how terrible—I did in the
name of love. How beautiful everyone was those days!
I had quick pulses in every part of me—my blood went
skyrocketing in all directions. . . . But now . . . I

wonder. . . . (*He takes his own pulse.*) Nothing . . .
Come on.

RONALD (*His alarm growing*)
Where?

STANLEY
You know where.

RONALD
I don't want to.

STANLEY
Come on, I say.

RONALD
No.

STANLEY
Just to look.

RONALD
No.

STANLEY
Just a little peek, that's all!

RONALD (*His terror is full now.*)
No—please!

STANLEY
Come on—he won't hurt you.

111

RONALD

I can't look at him!

STANLEY

Why?—he's in that chair. He hasn't moved—he never says a word! How can he hurt you?

RONALD

I don't know!

STANLEY (*Trying to comfort*)

Come on, Ronald—I'll protect you, really I will.

RONALD

I can't!—he scares me!

STANLEY (*Exasperated*)

Scares you?—why?—he's the same old Marco!

RONALD

He's not the same old Marco!—he's gone strange!

STANLEY

No!—there's nothing strange about him except he's sitting in a chair and not talking, which, I must say, is an enormous relief! Now come on!

RONALD

I won't!

STANLEY (*Grabbing him*)

I said come on!

RONALD

No—let me go! (*Raging and a little hysterical*) I won't go with you! I won't do anything you say! I won't vote for fire, I won't!

STANLEY

We don't care how you vote! It's Marco!—how *he* votes!—and you're going to help!

RONALD

Help?—how can I help?!

STANLEY

With him, with him!

RONALD

Me?—what good am I? He never paid any attention to me before!—why should he now?!

STANLEY

Because you're innocent!

RONALD

I'm what?!

STANLEY

Innocent!

RONALD (*Wild*)

I'm not!—no, I'm not!

STANLEY (*Pouncing*)
Ah!—you're guilty then!

RONALD (*Utterly fugitive now*)
Of what?

STANLEY (*The finger of accusation*)
Your mother!

RONALD
I'm not guilty of my mother!

STANLEY
Is she guilty of you?

RONALD
I didn't say that!

STANLEY
What are you guilty of?

RONALD (*Routed*)
I have to think, I have to think!

STANLEY
Think of your father!

RONALD
I did think of my father!

STANLEY
Then why are you guilty!?

114

RONALD

I am not guilty of my father!

STANLEY

Then *he* is!

RONALD

No, he's not guilty, no!

STANLEY

Then you are!

RONALD

No! It wasn't my fault!

STANLEY

Was it your mother's fault?!

RONALD (*An outcry*)

Does it have to be anybody's *fault?!*

STANLEY

Of course it does! Who did it?

RONALD

Did what, did what?!

STANLEY

Whatever was done!

RONALD

I don't know what was *done!*

STANLEY

You mean nothing was done?!

RONALD

Was there anything that *could* have been done?

STANLEY

My God, man, you mean you didn't *do* anything?

RONALD

I didn't know what to *do!*

STANLEY

And you didn't do *anything!?*

RONALD (*Breaking down*)

No, I didn't do anything. When I should have, I couldn't. When I could have, I wouldn't. When I would have, I didn't. I didn't do anything, I didn't do anything!

STANLEY

Then you're guilty!

RONALD

Yes!!

STANLEY (*Suddenly quiet, with serene logic*)

Why are you guilty if you didn't *do* anything?
(*Silence. Slowly* RONALD *turns his head.*)

RONALD

You mean I'm not guilty?

116

STANLEY (*With a smile*)

Not at all.

RONALD (*Slowly, slowly smiling*)

Then I'm . . . innocent.

STANLEY

Exactly what I said.

RONALD

Oh thank you, Stanley, thank you. (*He kisses* STANLEY's *hand. Then he starts to lick it.*)

STANLEY

Don't lick me, please. . . . I said don't lick me! (*He pulls his hand away.*) Now come on.
   (RONALD *sticks his tongue out and starts to caress his tongue with his fingers.*)

STANLEY

Stop doing that and come on.

RONALD

(*He stops caressing his tongue. He speaks wanly.*)
I want to see the little puppies. (*He caresses his tongue again.*)

STANLEY

I said stop doing that.

RONALD

The puppies. (*Caresses his tongue*)

STANLEY

Stop doing that disgusting thing with your fingers!

RONALD

If I could see the puppies . . . (*Caress*)

STANLEY

Stop it! (*After a moment, interested*) What puppies?

RONALD

I used to have a dog and one day I noticed her breast;
were getting larger and larger and larger.
(*He pauses.* STANLEY *waits for him to go on.
He doesn't.* STANLEY *is annoyed. He speaks with
irritation.*)

STANLEY

Well, that happens, you know—it happens all the time!

RONALD

Oh yes, larger and larger—until her titties started drag-
ging on the ground. And one night—while I was asleep
—I could hear her crying somewhere. I got out of bed
and went looking for her but I couldn't find her. Outside, inside, upstairs, down—I could hear her whining
and whining. Then, down the old cellar steps . . . and
there she was in the dark corner. And there, on the cellar
floor, all the pink around her, that wet pink, and the wet
white cord. One puppy . . . and she would bite the
cord and chew it and then lick him clean of bits of blood
and whiteness and wet. And another puppy . . . and
another. And then I touched one. (*With a little guilty*

118

pleasure) I held it in my hands and . . . pink and wet and warm and squirmy . . . lovely and warm and wet . . . and . . . (*The pleasure is too much for him. He starts to caress his tongue again.*)

STANLEY (*Unsteadily*)

Stop that!

    (RONALD *stops. He studies* STANLEY *ever so quietly.*)

RONALD

. . . Have you ever eaten a little puppy?

STANLEY (*Caught despite himself*)

. . . Alive?

    (RONALD *laughs very softly. Slowly, deliberately, he starts to caress his tongue again.*)

STANLEY

I said stop it!

RONALD

(*He stops, studies* STANLEY *a moment. Then, gently*) Could I touch your tongue?

STANLEY

Touch my what?

RONALD

Your tongue.

STANLEY
(*Jumping up. Trying to maintain his dignity*)
No!—certainly not! Touch my—?! No!

RONALD
Please, Stanley—could I touch it just once?

STANLEY
No—stop it!—get away from me!

RONALD
I won't pinch it or anything! I just want to touch it and
—and—kind of smooth it out, like!

STANLEY (*Apoplectic*)
Smooth it out? What makes you think it needs to be
smoothed out?! Get away from me, get away!

RONALD
Stanley—just touch it a little—caress, kind of—

STANLEY (*An outcry of righteous rage*)
You can't do that to me! You're innocent!—you're innocent! I'm the guilty one! I'm the one who gets to do
things like that!—you can't do that to me!
(STANLEY *is fugitive;* RONALD, *in pursuit.* JASON
enters. STANLEY *rushes behind* JASON.)

STANLEY
Jason—stop him!—keep him away from me!

JASON

What's going on?

RONALD

I won't hurt him!

JASON

Stop it, Ronald! Whatever's going on—stop it!
(*As* RONALD *tries to get by him*)
I said no more!
(RONALD *desists and goes sulking back to his toys.* STANLEY *neatens his clothes as if he has been attacked.* JASON *studies each of them briefly, then calls offstage.*)

JASON

Wheel him in!
(RONALD *and* STANLEY *instantly come to life, jumping up to watch the approach of the wheelchair.* SARAH *pushes the wheelchair.* DELIA *walks along one side of the chair;* WALTER, *along the other. It is a quiet, formal, solemn procession. The music is not electronic; it is traditional and stately. All eyes are fixed tensely on* MARCO *who sits in the chair, totally immobile, expressionless, his eyes vacant. The procession comes to a stop. Absolute stillness for a moment. Then:*)

JASON (*Gently, to* MARCO)
It's almost evening. How do you feel, Marco? (*Silence*)
Do you feel any better? (*Silence*) A little? You look

quieter, Marco—certainly quieter. Don't you feel some-
what improved? (*Silence.* JASON *turns to the others.*) I
think he *looks* a little better, don't you?

DELIA

He looked better when *I* was taking care of him!

SARAH (*Hotly*)

He did no such thing!

WALTER

He looked the best when I was pushing his chair!

SARAH *and* DELIA

When you were pushing his chair?! . . . You didn't
push it!—you hardly moved it at all!

JASON (*Stopping the argument*)

That's enough!
    (*Attention shifts back to* MARCO.)
If you don't want to tell us how you're feeling, perhaps
you'd like to talk of other things. Would you, Marco?
(*Looking off in the direction of* MARCO's *stare*) Ah yes,
that's Cassiopeia—all of that. And that's Orion, I think.
Yes, it *is* a lovely night—and windless, just as you say.

DELIA

He didn't say anything.

JASON

What?

I didn't hear him say a damn thing.

JASON (*Conspiratorially, to* MARCO)
Tell her, Marco. You and I have silent colloquies. We do,
don't we? (*With sharper insistence*) Don't we, Marco!
(*An instant, then:*) You know you'll have to speak, Marco
—sooner or later—you will! If it's to be fire, Marco—
you're the one I need! You're my tinder, my touchwood!
And I refuse to win this battle by some petty default!
Speak, Marco! (*With a laugh*) You can't win by simply
being absent, you know!—you won't get away with
that! You can't get away with getting away!—there's
no place to go to!—there are only distances! That's what
your eyes are seeing now, Marco—only distances! Look
at my hand!—that's *something!* There's no neutrality,
Marco—there's nothing between yes and no!—there's
only nothing! If you really want to say no, you have to
say it!—it's an action! (*He reaches into* RONALD'S *pouch
and takes out a toy knife.*) Here—even if it's only a toy
—stab somebody! Stab yourself! (*He tries to put the
knife into Marco's hand. The knife clatters to the floor.*)
Here—this is no toy—kill yourself! (*He reaches into his
pocket, pulls out a revolver and offers it to* MARCO.) Take
it, Marco—take it!
    (MARCO *doesn't move.* JASON *momentarily loses
    control.*)
Take it!—talk to me!—look at me!—say something!
            (*Silence*)

STANLEY
May I try him?

Go ahead.

STANLEY (*Good-naturedly, with friendliness*)
Marco, I don't mean to offend you, but what you're
doing is perversity, my friend. Pure perversion.

SARAH (*Relishing the irony*)
Pure perversion! What a lovely expression!

STANLEY
Pure and simple! What is perversion?—only a turning
away, that's all. And take my advice, old chum, there's
no good in that. I've tried them all. Homosexuality for
an easy start. But these days, that's no turn, that's straight
ahead. I've tried all sorts of fancies and fetishes. Sadism,
for example, and masochism, but which is which?—like
eating steak tartare—who's eating whom? Ah yes, I've
tried the arts. Painting the picture and dancing the
gavotte and doting so divinely on myself. And I do admit that, as perversions go, art is one of the dear narcis-
sistic delights. But oh, the dreadful day when the unreal
man in the looking glass spits very wetly in your very
real eye! I've even tried the dead. But the dead and the
living are opposite ends of the same worm. And when
you get to look squarely at your own tail end, what
a humiliating confrontation! Once, in nearly terminal
emergency, I tried liberalism. It was so cozy to love the
world and love the world and love the world and never
stir my stumps—but ultimately it felt like sucking a
nipple that had no breast attached. So take my word,
the best and last perversity—stay alive, go straight and

face it! There's everything in it, lad—sadism, masochism,
blood that never cleanses, all the swish and swagger of
the arts, empty nipples to suck and, finally, delicious
desperation and dearly beloved death! So straighten up,
boy—come alive!

(*Silence.* JASON *steps between* STANLEY *and*
MARCO.)

JASON

Go get it, Stanley.

STANLEY
(*An instant of puzzlement, then:*)
What, you mean it?

JASON
Yes.

(STANLEY *goes.*)
We go back to the rat, Marco. You don't know whether
the rat was real, do you? And you don't know whether
you want it to have *been* real. Anyway, the pain is over
and what've you got in its stead? This? Is this what you
want? No, man, you have got to *want!—you can't not
want!*

(STANLEY *returns wheeling a cart. It is a cross
between a hospital cart and a tea cart—white.
On it, a huge apothecary jar containing a
milky, murky fluid in which, a rat. Also, on the
cart, some tureens.*)
Ah, what is this? A tea cart, a pastry wagon? Not on
your life! (*He holds up the jar.*) Here it is—your rat!
You don't believe it's real? Study it. See the lips pulled

back, the rodent teeth, the slithery slimy tail. This fetid liquid—it's the mucous brine of the animal. Not real? Put your hand in the bottle, boy! See?—wetness! Touch it! Smell it! Now!—where'd the beast come from? Your gut? Are you sure? Where's the incision?—is there a scar? Was there a parturition?—do men breed rats? Or was it a dream, Marco? You didn't have it, you didn't lose it! Then what did you lose? Objective reality, what? Was it an organ?—did you lose an organ? Which one? A heart? (*Expansively*) Well then, my dear fellow, let's get you a new one! Man, we have everything— here, have a new heart! (*He reaches into a tureen and pulls out a bloody heart.*) Look at it—palpitating!—ticking against the tocks of time! Waltz time, march time, any time you like! If it's pain you want, this'll agonize, I promise you that! See a pretty sunset and it'll skip a hemidemisemiquaver, yes it will! It'll break and mend, break and mend a hundred times between kissings and killings! You want it?—cheap! (*He puts the heart down and holds up a brain.*) How about a brain? A little one, a big one, it doesn't matter—we make them standard now and quickly interchangeable—like cartridges! This object here—it used to be the style to want them deeply fissured, richly configurated. No more. The style is now for smooth ones. It's hard to sell a brain all wrinkled up with thought—people want the smooth unruffled surface. And take my word for it, once you've got one that's deeply fissured, it's hell to smooth it out again. (*He tosses the brain back.*) Which organ was the rat, my friend? What?—this one?! You want it?—we'll get you one!—as proud as a parapet! It'll stand so proudly at attention that it'll be mistaken for a man! (*Angry*)

What do you want, man?—what did you lose? Your soul?!

(*A look of pain crosses* MARCO'S *face.*)

There! He moved!

SARAH

I didn't see anything!

JASON

He did! When I said soul, he moved! Which one of these is your soul, Marco?—this one? (*He opens another crock. It is empty.*) Empty! (*Indicating the cart*) Take it away, Ronald. Say goodbye to it, Marco—it's gone. You'll never have that pain again. Question: What've you got in its place?

LORNA (*Entering*)

Loss.

JASON

What?

LORNA

The beloved loss.

JASON

No! There'll be no grieving! We'll have no such divertissements. Tell him that!

LORNA

Tell him yourself!

127

JASON

Talk to him, Lorna—make him come alive!

LORNA (*With a smile*)

How alive need he be?

JASON (*Pointing to* MARCO)

Is that enough life for you?

LORNA (*Enjoying* JASON's *discomfiture*)

Is it enough for him?

JASON

Look at him!

LORNA (*With a mocking smile*)

Look at you. As between the two of you—him flaccid
and you flailing—who's to know what's the most fitting
vivacity? Now study him: Life being what it is, that
may be just the right amount of liveliness!

JASON

No!—he's not alive at all!

LORNA

Ask him!

JASON (*Going to* MARCO)

Marco, are you alive enough? Give me your hand!
(*As* MARCO *doesn't respond,* JASON *seizes his
hand.*)

128

Damn you, give me your hand! (*To* LORNA) White—
soft—limp! Look how quickly a man's hand turns into
five white slugs! I can toss it back into his own face!
(*Which he does.*) Look at that mouth! That mouth
could utter a word that would drive me cringing back
into a cave!—why doesn't it? (*Whirling back to* MARCO)
Tighten the muscles of your mouth, you bastard! Here!
—take your pain back!
> (*He strikes* MARCO *a slashing blow across the
> mouth, then another and another. When he
> moves away, we see* MARCO *again, slumped to
> one side, blood rushing from his mouth.*)

SARAH *and* LORNA
Oh, he's bleeding! . . . Marco—Marco!
(*They both rush to help him.*)

LORNA
No—let me—let me!

SARAH
He's my son!—let me!

WALTER
I'm his father! I can take care of him!

DELIA
Here—let me wipe his mouth!

Stop fighting over him!—let me do it!

(Desperate, JASON *rushes down to the audience and speaks out in a flood of rage.)*

JASON

You! You fraud out there!—you cheapjack liar! Here's your chance!—bring him alive! Seduce him back to life! Come on—do it—you've got lots of ways! Hang a little carrot of hope in front of his face—that's always a good way! Make him a couple of rosy promises! Give him a little soft, sweet-smelling pillow of love! Tell him sunshine!—no rain today, no pain on Friday! Give him a pill!—yes, grind some little fantasy into a powder and roll it up into a little pill!—encapsulate the dream! Make magic!—give him wonders and witches! Burn a handful of mud in a glass alembic and let him watch it bubble and boil and turn green and purple and red and gold— then whisper in his ear all the dark alchemical meanings! Make an equation for him and give him a high, dry comfortable seat on the equal sign! Or make him merry— amuse him!—that's it, amuse him! Give him bright colors to play with, make sounds and movements in the wind, titillate him with small passions and pastimes, draw blood, make war, bedevil the deviate, bring on the clown!—make him laugh till he cries, *amuse him! (He looks back at* MARCO, *who is unchanged. He turns front again. With contempt:)* Look at him—no smile, not a simper's worth. Still dead without being dead. . . . And so are you. All this time we've been killing you—and still not dead? You old scrag, aren't you ashamed to hang on when nobody wants you? *Shame!* (*He spits, front.*) Die! Why don't you die? *Die!!* (*An instant, then the rage momentarily leaves* JASON; *momentarily he's forlorn and beaten. He turns to* MARCO *and speaks with deep sadness.*) Please, Marco—come to life! (*Silence. He turns to* LORNA *and speaks softly.*) Make love to him.

LORNA (*Quietly*)

No.

JASON (*Very gently*)

Are you content with him like that?
(*An instant. Then* LORNA *goes to* MARCO.)

LORNA

Marco . . . Marco, the sun has set. It's twilight—soon it'll be night. Soon, Marco. (*Touching her dress.*) This was made by worms—daytime, by worms; soon, at nighttime, it'll be silk. (*Indicating her pearls*). These—daytime, they were a sickness in the sea; nighttime—pearls! Look at me, Marco—touch me—smell me. Do you recall the reek of illness on me?—soon I'll be the perfume of the night! Soon, Marco—if the stars aren't too bright and the moon's on the wane a little—soon I'll be beautiful and the world will be bearable and you will love me! You will come alive and love me!
(*Silence. No sign from* MARCO)

DELIA (*Dryly*)

He doesn't even know she's there.

131

LORNA

Yes he does!

SARAH

He doesn't *show* he knows.

LORNA

He shows to me!

WALTER

Let her alone! Go on, Lorna—go on!

LORNA *(More desperate now)*

Marco, listen!—do you hear me, love? They say night and day are part of the same thing. Why, if they are, then nothing's tolerable! *(Confused)* I—something's wrong—a star—I've lost my place—

JASON

Moonlight—love—a star—

LORNA

—flew to fragments—

JASON

No! Love—stars—

LORNA

—fragments—no sense trying to put the pieces together again! Except by nighttime—

JASON (*Angry*)

Love, I said!

LORNA

Love me, Marco!

JASON (*Relaxing*)

That's it!—back on the track again!

LORNA

Love me! Look at me! Say something to me! Anything!
Tell me how beautiful I am! Tell me ugly! Tell me I'm
unclean! My breath's revolting—the morning muck is in
the corner of my eyes! Say it! (*Silence*) Well, my friend,
I'll say a thing or two to you! You and your petty aches
and petulances—you make me sick! I am so bored with
playing the fool to you! And hearing your eternal verities! Verities, my ass! It's lower mathematics! Rational
numbers—mean little means and medians—while the tears
roll down the cellar stairs! Hold me in your arms! Please!
—hold me!

> (*Slowly, painfully* MARCO *raises his right fore-
> arm before his face. His palm faces us; the back
> of his hand lightly touches his forehead, cover-
> ing his right eye. He may be shutting out the
> pain of the light; or, he may be fending off the
> painful sight of* LORNA'S *pleading. A general
> excitement in the room.*)

ALL EXCEPT JASON

Look—he moved! . . . His arm—look at his arm! . . .
He's moving! Marco—Marco!

133

LORNA

You see that?—he moved!

WALTER

Yes!—he raised his arm!

SARAH

Yes!—as if to fend her off!

LORNA (*An outcry*)

No, not for that reason! The light was in his eyes!

DELIA

He's not moving any more!

LORNA

Marco!—say something—please!

DELIA

You've lost him again!

LORNA

Marco—Marco—

STANLEY

You'll never get to him that way!

LORNA

Yes I will! . . . Marco!

STANLEY

Not with talk you won't. Why don't you kiss him?

134

LORNA

Stay out of this!

STANLEY

You better kiss him. He's miles away and getting further all the time.

LORNA

He's not! He saw me!—he knew who I was!

STANLEY

You want him really to see you?—grab his hand!—put it on your breast!

DELIA *(Stepping forward)*

Let me do it!

LORNA

You stay away from him! I'll do it myself!
> (*She takes one of* MARCO's *hands;* DELIA *snatches his other hand.*)

Let go of him!

DELIA

I will—the minute you do something!

LORNA

Jason!—make her let go!

STANLEY *(To* LORNA*)*

You fool!—put his hand on your tit!

LORNA (*Letting* MARCO's *hand go*)
Stop it! Jason, tell them to stop it! You're loathesome,
all of you!
> (*While she has been talking,* DELIA *has taken*
> MARCO's *hand and places it on her own breast.*
> LORNA *sees.*)

No!—stop that!—stop!
> (STANLEY *steps squarely in* LORNA's *way, pro-*
> *tecting* DELIA's *activity.* LORNA *whirls back to*
> JASON.)

Jason—stop them!

JASON (*Quietly*)
Don't interfere, Lorna.

LORNA (*To* JASON)
How can you let her do that?!

JASON
If you can't stand to look at it, turn away!

LORNA
You want to get him that way?

JASON
What way, then?
> (LORNA *turns her back to the group. She*
> *weeps quietly. All eyes are on* DELIA. *She holds*
> MARCO's *hand to her breast. Doesn't move.*
> *Silence. Stillness.*)

136

STANLEY (*To* DELIA)

What are you going to do?—just stand there?—with his hand glommed onto you like that?

DELIA (*Sure of herself*)

That's right.

STANLEY

No activity?

DELIA (*She knows her business.*)

Not yet.

STANLEY

It's not very enterprising of you.

DELIA

I know what I'm doing! I trust my bosom to do my bosom's job!

WALTER

Well said! (*To* STANLEY) You let her alone! She's back to basics! Something you don't know about!

STANLEY (*With umbrage*)

Oh, don't I! Once, when I was sick of all my baroque pleasures, I tried the most bizarre one of them all!

WALTER

What's that?

STANLEY

A girl. Basics, you say? What a disappointment! When

it was over, she left the bedroom, went into the kitchen, opened the refrigerator, got herself an orange and, while peeling it, squatted on the kitchen floor and piddled. So much for basics.

WALTER

Squatted on the kitchen floor, did she? And piddled?

STANLEY

Yes!

WALTER

I wonder if she meant it as an affront.

RONALD (*Pointing to* DELIA)

Look! Look what she's doing!
(*A fixed expression on her face,* DELIA *is slowly, methodically rubbing* MARCO's *hand on her bosom.*)

STANLEY (*To* RONALD)

What's the matter with you?

RONALD (*Upset*)

Look what she's doing, look what she's doing!

STANLEY

She's got his hand on her bosom.

RONALD

She's rubbing it!

138

STANLEY

Of course she is!

DELIA (*To* MARCO)

There now, there now. Like it? Do you like it? Soft, isn't it? Oh yes, very soft. Just keep doing that and it'll start firming for you. You feel it firming now? You feel something, do you? Try the other now.

STANLEY

Put his other hand on your leg.

RONALD

No—no—stop that!

STANLEY (*To* DELIA)

Go on—on your leg.

DELIA

Yes. I think I will.
>   (*She does so.* RONALD *is repelled and excited.* WALTER *is horrified and excited.* JASON *is wry, somewhat detached and a bit forlorn.* SARAH *is viewing this as if it were a painful but necessary ordeal for* MARCO. LORNA *is entirely turned away from the group.* STANLEY *is clinically amused.*)

STANLEY

How is it, Marco—how's it feel?

DELIA (*With a giggle*)

I'm feeling it all—I don't think he's feeling anything—I'm feeling it all!

139

STANLEY

Put his hand higher up.

DELIA

How do you mean?

STANLEY

On your leg, on your leg! Here—I'll do it.
    (*He puts* MARCO's *hand higher up on* DELIA's
    leg.)
There!—that better?—sure it is! How about this?
    (*He puts* MARCO's *hand up under* DELIA's *skirt.*)
There!—how's that feel?
            (*Puts* MARCO's *hand still higher*)
And that—how's that feel?

DELIA

Oh lovely!

STANLEY

I'm not asking you! Marco—how's it feel?

DELIA

Higher—put it higher!

STANLEY

Marco, how's it feel, what color does it feel? (*Getting
excited at last*) Does it feel white or blue or pink?

RONALD (*Transported*)

Yes—pink!—it feels pink!

140

STANLEY

And is it soft—soft?

RONALD

Yes—soft!—it's soft! (*He is in an ecstasy of pleasure and pain.*) I can't stand it! Fire! I vote for fire!

(MARCO *pulls his hands away! But it is almost unnoticed in the commotion.* LORNA *for the first time turns. As* WALTER *turns to attack* RONALD, JASON *grabs the boy protectively and holds him away from* WALTER. STANLEY *howls with triumphant laughter.*)

WALTER (*To* RONALD)

You fool!

JASON

Let him alone!

SARAH

It's monstrous!—no!—he doesn't mean it!

ALMOST
UNISON

STANLEY

Another vote!—we've got another vote!

WALTER

I'll kill the boy! I'll kill him!

JASON

Hands off, Walter—get away from him!

DELIA (*An outcry*)
He moved! He moved again!

WALTER
Did he?

TOGETHER

SARAH
I didn't see it!

JASON
Are you sure?

DELIA (*Unable to control herself*)
Yes! He pulled his hands away from me! When Ronald
said fire, Marco pulled away!

JASON (*Excited*)
Yes, I'm sure he did! (*To* MARCO) Are you playing us
for idiots, Marco?—are you? Well, while you do—
behold, my friend—another vote! Change and change
and all worlds change! It's now Stanley, Ronald, Delia
and myself—and soon it'll be the others—and I'm con-
vinced you did move a little! Move the whole way,
Marco! Say fire!
(*Silence. In the quiet,* SARAH *laughs softly, com-
passionately. Everyone looks at her.*)

SARAH
You great big men. You think we make great decisions
for great reasons. Nonsense. It's the little things. Does
anyone have a toy?

142

WALTER

A toy?

SARAH

Yes. It isn't the bread that makes the pudding, it's the one
drop of vanilla. Does anyone have a toy?
(WALTER *steps forward. They become husband
and wife, father and mother. They treat each
other with calculated consideration.*)

WALTER

Now, Sarah dear, he's not a child.

SARAH (*With a faraway smile*)

He'll always be a child to me, Walter.

WALTER

You do worry over him too much, my dear.

SARAH

Is there a way of avoiding it?

WALTER

It's all in the way you think about it.

STANLEY

Gabble, gabble.

WALTER

A man grows up, you've got to let him grow.

143

SARAH

A child is a child—

WALTER

He's got to take on responsibilities—

SARAH

—is a child—

WALTER

—face the facts, look reality in the eye—

STANLEY

Gabble, gabble.

SARAH

—is a child, is a child—

WALTER

—be a citizen of the world—

SARAH

—is a child, is a child—

STANLEY

Gabble, gabble.

WALTER

—head and shoulders above the rest, shoulder to the
wheel, shoulder—uh—shoulder—

STANLEY (*A military command*)
Arms!

WALTER (*The drill officer!*)
Shoulderrrrr—

STANLEY
Arms!

WALTER (*Very crisp*)
How many shoulders?

STANLEY (*Saluting*)
Nineteen, sir!

WALTER
How many arms?

STANLEY
Eleven, sir! Hands and fingers attached!

WALTER
Detach them!

STANLEY
One detachment!

WALTER
Any other arms?

STANLEY
Arm-*chairs*, sir!

145

WALTER

Send three. Any other arms?

STANLEY

Arm-pits, sir!

WALTER

Send fifteen. What else?

STANLEY

Armageddons.

WALTER

Send two. No. One's enough—save the other!

STANLEY

Yes, sir.

WALTER

Anything else?

STANLEY *(Pointing to* MARCO)

Him, sir.

WALTER

Send him!

SARAH

No! I won't let you send him!

STANLEY

Ah—saved!

146

WALTER

No one will be saved! Salvation is for fools!

SARAH

I'll save him! (*To* MARCO) I won't let them take you! I promise I won't! You're too young. You're my baby, you're my baby! Go on, suck your fingers, baby!—suck your fingers the way Ronald does—go on! (*She puts* MARCO'S *fingers in his mouth.*) Ronald, give him one of your toys.

RONALD

I'll give him one of my fingers.

SARAH (*Annoyed*)

No! One of your toys, please!

RONALD

No.
        (JASON *picks up* RONALD'S *pouch of toys.*)
Jason—please—they're mine!

JASON (*To* SARAH)

Here, mother.

SARAH

Don't you dare to call me mother! (*Indicating* MARCO) This is my only son! (*She starts selecting toys for him.*) There, darling, you just go on sucking your fingers and mother will find you a toy. Here—here's a lovely box.

147

Would you like to have it? (*She puts it on his lap.*) Go on—open it—open it! Well, naughty boy, I'll do it for you then.

(*She opens the box and a hideous toy snake pops out and hits him in the face. He doesn't stir. Everybody laughs—except* LORNA *and* JA-SON. SARAH *laughs the loudest.*)

There—wasn't that funny? Didn't you die of amusement? Here—here's another one. It's a kaleidoscope. Look in—look in and see all the beauteous colors of the world! (*Rhapsodically*) Look in—look in!

(*She holds it up to his eyes and squeezes. A stream of orange-colored ink squirts into his eyes. She squeezes again. A stream of purple this time. It pours down his face. He remains totally impassive.*)

Laugh, darling!—why don't you laugh? Isn't it funny? Didn't it kill you, didn't it murder you? (*With sudden pity for him*) Oh, my poor darling, what can I do if I can't make you laugh! (*She starts to wipe his face with her handkerchief.*) Go on—suck your fingers, darling. Does anyone have a toy for him? Go on, sweet angel, suck your fingers. (*Weeping now*) Please—doesn't anybody have a toy?!

(*Silence.*)

DELIA

I have one.

(*Slowly, while all the others are still,* DELIA *takes a few steps back into the darkness. All eyes follow her. She returns with a large doll. It looks very much like* DELIA *herself. It is*

148

dressed in a costume identical to DELIA'S. *She holds it tenderly, with deep affection.*)

RONALD

Why, it's a doll!

DELIA (*Quietly*)

Yes, it's mine.

RONALD

A boy can't have a doll!

STANLEY (*Withering* RONALD)

Don't be ridiculous!

DELIA

(*Gently, even a little tenderly, to* SARAH)

He may have it. Will you give it to him?

SARAH (*Unsurely*)

I'm not sure it *is* the right thing for a little boy.

WALTER

Sarah—give it to him. Don't hurt Delia's feelings. It's very dear to her. Isn't it, Delia?

DELIA (*Loath to part with it*)

Yes. And it's not an ordinary doll. It's very pretty, as you can see. And it does everything. It eats and it sleeps. It dances a little and it cries. And it says "I love you" and it . . . dies.

149

SARAH   (*Gently, moving toward* DELIA)
It dies, does it? How clever it is! Here, Marco.
(*She takes the doll from* DELIA, *crosses back to*
MARCO *and puts the doll in* MARCO's *lap. An
instant, then* SARAH *lets out a scream.*)
Oh no! Look! (*She points to* MARCO's *lap.*) Look at what
she's doing! She's wetting! That nasty little doll is
wetting! She's wetting his trousers!

DELIA
I told you she does everything!

(SARAH *snatches the doll off* MARCO's *lap and
throws the doll savagely on the floor at* DELIA's
feet.)

SARAH
You bitch! You dirty little bitch! (*She flies back to*
MARCO.) Here, let me dry you—let me dry you, poor
darling! (*With her handkerchief again, she starts wiping*
MARCO's *lap. While doing this:*) Oh, wet all over—my
poor angel! Let that be a lesson to you—never trust a
woman! Mother's the only lady you can trust! Go on—
suck your fingers, sweetheart! Suck your fingers, love!
They're all bitches, you know—they'll do this to you
every time! Suck your fingers, sweetheart. Oh angel—
love!—let me kiss you!—let me kiss you! (*She kisses him
passionately and rapidly—his forehead, his cheeks, his
lips, his hands.*) Come on—say you love me—say you
love mother—say it! Wait! I have something special for
you!—oh, very special for you! (SARAH *scurries back
into the darkness and returns almost instantly. She carries*

an uninflated toy balloon and a cylinder of gas.) Help
me! Someone help me! Walter! Stanley! Help me!

> (WALTER, STANLEY *and* RONALD *go to her assist-
> ance.*)

Now blow—all of you! Blow it up! Make it as large as it
will get!

> (*As she speaks, they adjust the cylinder and
> inflate the balloon with gas. It gets larger and
> larger.*)

Larger—larger! Keep blowing! Blow—blow! Blow it up
as large as it can be! Look at it, look at it!—soft at first,
but firming, firming—getting larger all the time! Oh,
look at it!

> (*The balloon is now four feet in size.*)

Don't stop—don't weaken, any of you—blow it up—
keep blowing!

> (*The balloon is four feet, five feet. The picture
> painted on it is getting clearer.*)

See how great it is! See how great and beautiful! See
how succulent it is!

> (*The painting on the balloon is clear—a huge
> breast.*)

Larger—greater—blow, blow!

> (*Sighs of admiration from the others. The
> breast is now huge.* MARCO *rises. Utter silence
> except for the sound of the gas cylinder.*)

Stop it! That's enough!

> (*The sound of the gas cylinder is stilled. Utter
> silence. As they all watch to see what* MARCO
> *will do, he bends down to pick something off
> the floor. Now, suddenly he rises—the flash of
> metal—he has* RONALD'S *knife in his hand!*)

No! Stop him! He has a knife! Stop him!
> (*Commotion! They all try to prevent* MARCO.
> *A skirmish! He drives the knife into the bal-
> loon. It explodes. It is gone. Left in* STANLEY'S
> *hand, like an obscene thing, the balloon skin,
> torn and dangling.*)

Oh no! Oh no!
> (*Her outcry is an agony. She doubles over as
> if* MARCO'S *thrust has gone into her own breast.
> In pain*)

Oh, hold me!—hold me! Oh, son—hold me!

JASON

Go to her—she wants you!

MARCO (*Quietly*)

No—you.

JASON

She's your mother!

MARCO

Yours!—you claimed her!

SARAH

Oh, son! One of you—one of you be my son!—hold me!
> (*She is in despair.* JASON *rushes to her side. But
> he doesn't touch her.*)

JASON

Say fire!

SARAH (*Weeping*)

No! Hold me—I may fall—

JASON (*As the others start for her*)

No—don't touch her—stand back, all of you! (*To* SARAH) Say it!

SARAH (*Weeping—barely audible*)

Fire—yes—fire!
(*He rushes to her and takes her into his supporting arms. As he leads her off:*)

SARAH

Oh my son! Oh Jason, my son! (*But the instant before she departs, her eyes turn back. Her outcry is full of compassion for him, and remorse over having betrayed him.*) Oh, Marco—forgive me—forgive me—
(*JASON leads* SARAH *off. The others go with them, except for* MARCO, LORNA *and* WALTER. MARCO *looks to the floor and picks up the remains of the balloon. As he stares at the obscene thing, he is filled with bewilderment and self-revulsion. Suddenly he snatches up a scrap of the balloon and stretches it across his face, sucking it in, gasping, trying to breathe through it. It is like a caul.*)

LORNA (*Gently*)

Here. I'll take that from you.

MARCO (*Sharply*)

No!

LORNA

I'll take it!
　　(*With sudden violence he snatches it away.*)

MARCO

No! (*He violently throws it on the floor.*) It's dead, it's gone! Come on, Lorna!

LORNA

Where?

MARCO

It's nighttime—look! It's dark enough to hide!
　　(*JASON enters.*)

JASON

Hide from whom, Marco?

MARCO

From you, for one! Come on, Lorna!
　　(*LORNA is painfully indecisive.*)

JASON

She doesn't want to go, do you, Lorna? She wants to stay here, where there's still a glimmer of light . . . and hear you say she's beautiful!

WALTER

And he will—he certainly will!

MARCO

Stay out of it, you romantic old idiot! Lorna, come on!

154

(She starts to go. JASON's voice stops her.)

JASON

Lorna—wait! What do you need his darkness for?—
you've got your own! You want to hear him say you're
beautiful, make him say it here—in the light—as he sees
you!

MARCO *(A cry)*

Lorna!
> *(He starts to go. LORNA calls, without moving after him.)*

LORNA

Marco—please!

MARCO

Damn you, Jason!

WALTER

He'll say it—in front of everybody!

MARCO

Stop it! *(To LORNA, pleading)* Come on—I beg you—

LORNA

Marco—it's only a word—like all the nonsense words—
a game!

JASON

No, it's a lie—isn't it, Marco!?

MARCO

Yes—no!

WALTER

It's not a lie! Tell her she's beautiful!

LORNA (*To* MARCO—*desperately*)

Not for my sake—for your own!

JASON (*Angry*)

It's not for his sake and you know it! The man's a fool
—he'll die if he lies to you! He has to make do with the
truth—he has to dole it out over all his hungers! (*Turning to* MARCO) Go on, Marco—try it—lie to her!

MARCO (*An outcry*)

It's not a lie!

WALTER

Good! That's a very good start!

JASON

Go on, then. Say she's beautiful!

MARCO

She's—

JASON

Don't look at me—look at her! Go on—say it!

LORNA

Hurry, Marco!

156

WALTER

Her eyes are starlight!

MARCO (*Quickly*)

Starlight, yes!

WALTER

She's dressed in white satin—

MARCO

—white satin, with a train—

JASON

No! Her dress is filthy—torn—it's full of holes!

LORNA

Don't listen to him!

WALTER

Her dress is moonlight—

LORNA

No—please!

WALTER

Made by a thousand nuns—

JASON

Made by worms!

MARCO

Silk—

JASON

Made by worms!

MARCO

Pearls—pearls—

JASON

A sickness in the sea—

MARCO

No!

JASON

Look at her! Sickness!

LORNA

No! *I* said that!

JASON

Yes, you did! (*To* MARCO) Sickness—sores—chancres
—kiss her—why don't you kiss her?!

LORNA

Oh, please, Marco!

JASON

Diseased!

LORNA

Say beautiful!

MARCO

Let me alone!

158

LORNA (*An outcry*)
Marco! (*She tries to hold him.*)

MARCO (*Breaking away*)
Let me alone! Oh, why do we see each other in the light?!

LORNA
Marco—no—Marco! Oh, let me be burnt! Fire! Fire!
(*She departs.*)

MARCO
The trial!—please!—the trial!

WALTER
You're an abomination!

MARCO
Is that the charge?

WALTER
Sarah loved you and Lorna was beautiful! You've made a mockery of women!

JASON
He's killed all his mothers!

MARCO
Oh, that's the charge, is it? (*Quickly, to* WALTER) But there are ten sides to everything, aren't there, Old Pomp and Circumstance?

WALTER

Don't you dare speak disrespectfully to me. I'm your father!

MARCO

Am I guilty of that too?

WALTER

You're guilty of everything!

MARCO

Ha!—first I'm guilty, then I'm on trial!

JASON

Is there a tidy order to these things?

MARCO

But I haven't testified—you haven't heard the evidence!

WALTER

Who has to hear the evidence?

JASON

The sentence is always the same!

MARCO

Then it's a mock trial after all!

JASON

It's certainly not real to anybody but you!

WALTER

It's forgotten before it's over!

160

JASON

It never properly begins!

WALTER

The execution often comes first! (*Calling*) Warden! Where's the executioner?

MARCO

No! I'll have my trial! I'll have my chance to testify!

WALTER

Warden!

JASON

Here, sir! (*He salutes.*)

MARCO (*With a wild realization*)

Oh, it's another game, isn't it? Count me in! Modella-doro!

WALTER

Warden!

JASON

Yes sir!

WALTER

Where's the executioner?

JASON (*Saluting again*)

Here, sir!

MARCO

Bellamirado! Simulacrum! No, that's a word!

WALTER

Is the prisoner tightly bound? Is he secure?

JASON

Are you tightly bound? Are you secure?

MARCO

Oh yes, nice and secure, thank you. Very comfy. Arra-pundra!

WALTER (*To* JASON)

Are your men all ready?

JASON

(*Saluting alternately with right and left, rapidly*)
Yes, sir! Here, sir! Right, sir!

WALTER

Are your men armed?

JASON

All armed, sir.

WALTER

Very well. (*Stentoriously*) Rea-deeeee!
    (WALTER *points imperiously to* JASON. JASON *raises both arms to make a "rifle" of them. Off-stage, the drum roll starts. Behind it, the wail of electronic music.* WALTER *raises his arm.*)
Ai-ai-aim!

162

(*The drum roll continues; the electronic music
increases in decibels.*)
And—

(WALTER *is about to drop his arm on the word
fire. The electronic music is deafening.* MARCO
breaks out of his position.)

MARCO

No—stop! Please!—stop! Nobody's heard the evidence!
(*Slowly, without saying the word,* WALTER
*lowers his arm. With the utmost commiseration,
he puts a gentle hand on* MARCO's *shoulder.*)

WALTER

I beg you—for your own heart's ease—don't try to
change it. The evidence may always be different and the
sentence forever the same, yet—have you any real hope
of changing it?

MARCO

Hope or no hope—

MARCO	
I'm afraid!	
	TOGETHER
JASON	
—he's afraid!	

(WALTER *looks quickly from one to the other
of them, a small scurry of fright across his
face.*)

WALTER (*Unsteadily*)

Are we—is it permitted—are we allowed to say that?

163

MARCO

What else can we *say?!*

WALTER (*In a flood of relief and terror*)

Then I'll say it too! Me too! Afraid! I'm terrified! I lock my doors at night—

JASON

Against what, old man?

WALTER (*An outcry*)

Oh, is it against you? I don't know! But I lock them! Oh, I thought terror was only for the old! And, world knows, I'm older than everybody! So I take precautions I never took when I was young! I give more alms to the poor! I fasten buttons against the slightest wind! I turn my collar often and I pray! But all of that —because I'm old! But the one comfort I have—is that you and you!—the young!—you are not afraid! And if you tell me that you too are fastening buttons against the wind—oh no, don't say that!—oh, help me! Marco, hide me! (*He throws himself into* MARCO's *arms.*) Hide me!

MARCO

(*Pushing him aside roughly so as to hide that he is moved by him*)
Get away!—let me alone.

WALTER (*Rushing to* JASON)

Jason—please—hide me, hide me!

JASON (*Quietly pushing him away*)

Get away from me! Your scare smells bad!

164

WALTER (*An outcry of rage*)
You need me to be scared! Just as I need you to be bold
and brave, you need me to be a coward! How else could
you ever kill me? Why, if I had one muscle in my body
that I could count on—with what I *know!*—I would
make rubble of both of you! (*In mountainous anger*)
But what you need me to be is a weak old man! So that
you can loathe me without feeling contempt for your-
selves, so that you can hide me from your friends and
my enemies! And so that, in the end, you can strike me
down and crow over my dead body—and be *heroes!* In
short, what you need me to be is your father!

MARCO
And you love me!

WALTER
Yes! Don't I let you kill me? What more do you want?!

MARCO
Confess me!

WALTER
. . . What?

MARCO
Be my father. Confess me.

WALTER (*With quiet dread, he turns to* JASON)
What does he mean, Jason?

165

JASON (*Quietly*)
He says be his father. Confess him . . . I say the same.
. . . Both of us.

WALTER (*With a frightened little laugh*)
Con—confess you? No—not that kind of father. You're
joking, of course . . . both of you.

MARCO
Confess me, Father, for I have sinned.

JASON
Confess me, Father, for I have sinned.

WALTER (*A cry of horror*)
No!
(*He starts to flee.* JASON *grabs him.*)

JASON
Stay here—you said you loved us!

WALTER
No—let me go!

MARCO
Confess us, Father.

WALTER (*Terrified*)
No—I won't stay here!

JASON (*Barring his flight*)
Oh yes you will! You'll stay. And you'll turn your collar
around and you—

166

WALTER

No!

(He starts to run from the room.)

MARCO *and* JASON *(Together)*

Stop! . . . Grab him!

*(A brief wild scuffle. JASON grabs WALTER and
pins the old man's arms behind his back.)*

WALTER

Let me go! Oh please!

JASON *(To MARCO)*

Turn his collar around!

WALTER

Oh no—oh please!

JASON

Turn his collar around!

*(As JASON holds him taut, WALTER trembles
and weeps softly, his head thrown back in
torment.)*

Hurry! Turn his collar around!

*(Silence. MARCO struggles within himself, then
slowly crosses the room and as gently as he can
he turns WALTER's collar around. JASON slowly
releases him. Very little opposition is left in the
old man.)*

JASON *(He gestures WALTER to a stool.)*

Sit down.

WALTER

No.

MARCO

Please sit.

WALTER

No—don't make me.

MARCO

Please sit . . . Father.
(WALTER *hears the name "Father."* . . . *Slowly,*
trembling, he sits on the stool. MARCO *pulls up*
a chair which he sets alongside the stool. It is a
high-backed wooden chair with many narrow
spindles. MARCO *kneels on the floor, his elbows*
on the chair-seat, his hands folded. He looks
through the spindles of the chair, at his con-
fessor. JASON *does not kneel. He stands behind*
MARCO.)

MARCO

Father, I have sinned.

WALTER

No—please—

JASON

Father, I have sinned.

WALTER (*Whimpering*)

Oh, stop it!

168

MARCO

I have been proud and unrepentant.

JASON

I've lied and I've cheated in the marketplace.

WALTER

There is nothing I can do!

MARCO

I have taken His name in vain.

JASON

I've borne false witness.

WALTER

You're in the wrong department.

MARCO

I've worshipped graven images. I've deluded myself with songs and artifacts.

JASON

I've feasted on fasting days.

WALTER

You're in the right building but the wrong department.

MARCO

I have been overly proud of words. I've boasted that there was grace in them.

JASON

I have been seduced by Things.

MARCO

I have been seduced by the Likenesses of things.

WALTER

Have you put in for a transfer, have you filled out an application?

MARCO

Father, listen to me!

WALTER

Have you followed all the forms, taken the proper procedures—

MARCO *and* JASON

Please listen! . . . Stop it!

WALTER

—filled out the questionnaire?

MARCO *and* JASON

What? . . . What questionnaire?

WALTER

Answer the question, if you please!

JASON

We're trying!

| TOGETHER

MARCO

What is the question?!

170

WALTER

How have you sinned?

MARCO

I've fallen in love with numbers. I've been bewitched
by magic. I've tried to make an alchemy of brain and
blood. I've spat into the face of God. I've coveted the
realm of heaven. Absolve me! Keep me from the flame!
Absolve me!

WALTER

Have you kept the Sabbath?

MARCO

Save me from the fire!—absolve me!

JASON

I've coveted my neighbor's wife!

WALTER

Have *you* kept the Sabbath?

MARCO

I have dishonored my—my—

JASON

—Father!

MARCO

Dishonored my Father!

171

WALTER

Ask God for forgiveness.

MARCO

I ask you!

WALTER

Ask God!

MARCO

God is not my relative!

WALTER

Am I then?

MARCO

I don't know!

WALTER (*Quickly*)

Is your mother?

MARCO

No!

JASON

Yes!

WALTER

Have you dishonored your mother?

MARCO

No!

172

JASON

Yes!

WALTER

She suckled you! Did she not suckle you!?

MARCO

No!

JASON

Yes!

WALTER

Did you take her breast in your mouth?

MARCO

No!

JASON

Yes!

WALTER

Was there comfort in it?—was there pleasure?—the felicities of flesh?

JASON

Yes!

(MARCO *jumps up from his kneeling position.*)

MARCO

No! No more of this!

173

(JASON *abruptly kneels into the position* MARCO
formerly held.)

JASON

Yes—comfort—felicity!

MARCO

Don't do it, Jason! Get up—get up!

WALTER (*To* JASON)

One breast suckled you and gave you sustenance! Did
you lay your hand on the other breast?

JASON (*In pain*)

I don't know! Yes, I did!

MARCO

Jason—

WALTER

Did you caress it?

JASON

Yes I did!

MARCO

Jason—get up!

WALTER

Did you touch her?

174

JASON (*Tormented*)

I said I did!

WALTER

Any other part of her?

JASON

Perhaps—by accident—

MARCO

Jason—stop!

WALTER

Did you want her?

JASON (*In torment*)

I didn't know I did!

WALTER

Did you want her, did you want her?! (WALTER *has suddenly turned upstage, his body hunched over.*) Answer me!—oh answer me!

MARCO

You lecherous old bastard!

WALTER

No—stop!

MARCO

You're not confessing him!

175

WALTER

I am—I am!

MARCO

You're playing with yourself!

WALTER

No!
> (MARCO *kicks the chair away and grabs* WALTER
> *by the throat. As he pulls the old man up,*
> *throttling him, he shouts:*)

MARCO

Everybody, come! Come, look at him with his fly open!
Playing with himself while confessing us! Everybody,
come!

WALTER *(In a wild outcry)*

Oh, stop him! Nothing is beautiful—stop him! Fire! Fire!
Jason! Fire!
> (JASON *rushes to them. He starts to pull* MARCO
> *away.*)

JASON

Stop it!—let him go!—let him go!
> (*He pulls them apart.*)

MARCO

Why did you stop me?

JASON

Because you want him alive!

176

MARCO

I do not want him alive!

JASON

Then why did you go on your knees to him? You were first!—why did you go on your knees to him? You love him more than I do! He's your father more than mine!
(*The others have all returned*—DELIA *first, then* RONALD, STANLEY *and* SARAH. LORNA, *the last.* JASON *points to the others.*)
And them—all of them—you need them all! They're all your relatives!—more than they're mine!
(MARCO *is berserk. He rushes from one to another of them.*)

MARCO

Relatives!—very well!—my relatives! Then help me! (*To* RONALD) You—Boy—help me! One of those toys! Your school—may I go to your school?

RONALD

Let me go!

MARCO

Help me!
(RONALD *moves away.* MARCO *rushes to* DELIA.)
You—you hold my hand! I find it impossible—impossible to keep—to keep my hands steady! My hands are shaking—hold my hands!

DELIA

I do not speak to strange men on the street.

177

MARCO

My sister! Someone said you were my sister!

DELIA

I truly don't recall!

MARCO

Yes—my sister! (*He rushes to* STANLEY.) You—can you —can you help?

STANLEY (*With dignity*)

What exactly is it you want?

MARCO

Some—I don't know—where to go—a place—why can't I touch someone without pain? Was it an error, to hope there would be order in this?—oh, let me hold your hand!

STANLEY (*Frightened*)

Get away from me!

MARCO

Please—let me hold your hand! (*He grabs* STANLEY'S *hand*)

STANLEY

Let me go! Let go my hand! Let go! (*Calling*) Officer! Officer!

   (WALTER *steps forward officiously.*)

178

WALTER
What is it?—what's going on here?

STANLEY
This man—he grabbed my hand—I think he's a degenerate.

MARCO
No, officer—no!

WALTER
(*Taking out an imaginary book and pencil*)
What is your name?

MARCO
I don't know. (*Pulling himself together to give the acceptable answer*) I've been away. I've been serving my country in the army, the navy, the marine and medical corps. I've been wounded many times. They've taken away my rat and given me nothing in its place!

WALTER
Oh, come now—new heart, new brain!

MARCO
I've lost my serial number, my address book, my membership card, my family Bible and photo album and all my cards of identity! Oh help me, I want to take a bus to—a bus to—

WALTER
I'm sorry, my good man. I never carry change with me.
(MARCO *rushes to* SARAH. *He is about to fall.*)

179

MARCO

Oh, could I rest with you? Please let me rest!

SARAH

Where?

MARCO

Anywhere. I just want to close my eyes. Go home. Put my head on your breast.

SARAH (*Quietly*)

Didn't you know? I've had my breasts removed. Everybody's doing it these days. It's . . . all the rage.

MARCO

Lorna! Lorna, where are you? (*He sees her.*) Lorna, are they my relatives? Why don't they take me in? I'm lost —where shall I go?

LORNA (*Quietly*)

I don't know. I'm a stranger here myself.
(*His last gasp—a savage outcry to the audience.*)

MARCO

You—you out there!—help me! You!—where are you! Don't run away! Stop! Stop! (*He reaches to the floor for the pistol.*) Stop! (*He shoots once, twice, again.*) Stop in the name of the—in the name of the—(*He starts to weep.*) Jason!! (JASON *hurries forward and takes him in his arms.* MARCO *continues to weep as* JASON *comforts him.*)

JASON (*With deep love and compassion*)

Come. Come, Marco—come. Weep, boy, weep. Weep, child. Weep, man. Don't you know I love you? Don't you know I've always loved you? Is there anyone who could love you more? Come now, let me wipe your tears away. Let me kiss your forehead. Don't you know I love you? Don't you know that I will hate you until the end, and love you? Look at me, Marco. Look into my eyes, dear Marco. Whom do you see? Let me look into yours. Whom do I see? Love me, Marco—as I love you. Say fire, my beloved, say fire.

MARCO (*Softly*)

Fire . . .

JASON

Again. Say it again. Stay close in my arms. Say it again.

MARCO (*More audibly now*)

Fire.

JASON

Call it out, my love. I love you, Marco. Call it out, my beloved.

MARCO

Fire—fire—fire!
(*He has come down to the footlights again. He is shouting it at the top of his voice, sobbing and exultant and terrified. The lights go to black.*)